The Healing of Marriage

The
Healing of Marriage

A PRACTICAL HANDBOOK OF
MARRIAGE COUNSELING

WILLIAM L. CARRINGTON, M.D.

CHANNEL PRESS · GREAT NECK · NEW YORK

THE HEALING OF MARRIAGE

Library of Congress Catalog Card Number: 61-17158

Contents

Preface

DR. WILLIAM CARRINGTON has thrice put me in his debt. Within minutes of my first meeting him in England in 1952, he lent me some money! (I had just arrived from the U.S.A., and had no sterling.) In 1956, on a lecture tour in Australia, I was taken ill, and he took me into his home and restored me to health. In 1958, while I was away on an extended project in Asia, he came to the United States and took over my teaching assignments at Drew University in New Jersey.

Out of these and other experiences, a deep understanding and friendship has grown up between us. In long hours of conversation, and in the sharing of conferences and case discussions, I have developed a profound admiration and respect for his insight, his competence, and his outgoing compassion toward people in trouble. He has an original, enquiring mind that will not be satisfied with superficial explanations, but must always be digging deeper in the search for root causes. He has a gift for lucid and persuasive communication which has made him an outstanding radio personality in his native Australia. Above all, he combines a scientific knowledge of his field, based on wide reading and study, with a mystical sensitivity to aesthetic and religious values. Few clinicians of my acquaintance have been able, as consistently as he has, to keep in such perfect balance the concept of the wholeness of man, as body, mind and spirit.

9

In his home in Melbourne Dr. Carrington has set up, with a group of medical colleagues, a flourishing experiment in group practice. He has devoted himself more and more, in recent years, to psychotherapy and marriage counseling. He is much in demand as a consultant in these areas. In addition, he has concerned himself actively with the promotion of marriage guidance in his own land; particularly in fostering the training of marriage counselors and in developing counseling courses for the clergy. When I visited Australia he met me at Sydney Airport in his official capacity as President of the National Marriage Guidance Council—an office he discharged with great distinction.

It would be hard to find a man better qualified than Dr. Carrington to write an introductory handbook of marriage counseling. Besides his experience in Australia, he has had intimate contact with developments in this field in Britain and in the United States. He has kept himself fully informed of the most recent developments, yet has preserved a healthy detachment from particular groups and schools of thought.

In this book he has provided us with a serviceable guide to a new and as yet ill-charted field. He has written simply, so that the beginner can follow him without effort. At the same time the experienced counselor will find, particularly in the later chapters, much that will stimulate his thought. In two areas—the relation between personality disorder and marriage, and the dynamics of interaction between counselor and client —his discussion seems to me to be particularly helpful.

The literature in the field of marriage counseling is as yet sparse. We have greatly needed a book such as this, and I warmly welcome its appearance. It is by no means the last word on the subject, as the author would readily concede. There are points of interpretation at which I would want to join issue with him, and launch into one of those long, exciting discussions which he and I have so much enjoyed in the past. But taken as a whole, the book is sound, well balanced, and practical. I have read it with much pleasure and profit, and express the hope that other readers will have the same rewarding experience.

DAVID R. MACE
Executive Director, American
Association of Marriage Counselors

Introduction

MARRIAGES, LIKE PEOPLE, can sicken and die. The sickness of marriage may be acute or chronic, mild or severe, general or limited to one aspect of the relationship, one part of the "body." It may be progressive or recurrent, obvious or hidden, comparable in all these respects with the sickness of persons.

The sickness or death of marriage, however, will generallly have wider and more far-reaching consequences than the sickness or death of persons. Mental illness, delinquency, vandalism, gangsterism, crime, alcoholism, "accident proneness," and many other distressing and costly social disorders can all too often be traced back to a kind of "psychic malnutrition" in childhood—to the deprivation of the kind of love and security that are as necessary for the development of stable personalities as food and fresh air are necessary for the development of stable bodies. The sickness and death of marriages may therefore be regarded as of national significance, perhaps even as the greatest internal threat to national stability.

Sick and broken marriages, like sick and broken persons, can be healed. Better still, such tragedies can often be prevented by better and more universal preparation for marriage and parenthood. The increasing realization of these great facts has led to rapidly expanding efforts in practically every country in the world to devise and carry out appropriate measures for the prevention—and healing—of marital disorders. These efforts form one of the great creative social enterprises of this twentieth century, and the present decade will certainly be marked by continuous development and expansion of all aspects of the work.

This book is mainly concerned with the healing of marriage through the kind of service known as marriage counseling. The aim has been to make it a practical handbook for the increasing numbers of people throughout the world who are equipping themselves and offering their services in formal marriage counseling, and also for those who may find themselves involved in less formal but serious attempts to help relatives, friends, clients, parishioners and patients in marital difficulties.

For the experienced marriage counselor, this volume may do little more than offer an interesting account of how another marriage counselor feels about the work. For the less experienced and more recently trained marriage counselor, and for counselors in training, it may prove a useful source for reference.

For people with little or no training or experience in marriage counseling who may at times be confronted by marriage partners in urgent need of help, and even for some married people in their own marital conflicts, it may, it is hoped, provide some fruitful ideas, and some guidance as to how such bewildering and distressing situations may be handled most effectively, or at least without doing harm.

But this is not intended in any way to be a "do it yourself" book. As will be clear from its contents, no book can make a good marriage counselor. But there does seem to be need for a book which offers some detailed practical help in the very delicate and complex work of marriage counseling, to supplement the training that counselors may have received or may be receiving, and possibly to inform interested people something of what marriage counselors seek to achieve and how they set out to do it.

For purposes of discussion the process of counseling as described in this book has been "taken to pieces" to some extent in a manner that would not generally happen in the actual practice of counseling. But although the various sections of the work would always tend to overlap and become mixed up with one another, the counselor needs to have some clear and balanced comprehension of where he is and what he is dealing with at any stage in the counseling, so that he can avoid being too much "caught up" in the possible confusion of the partners who seek his help.

In this artificial, yet logical, separation of the elements of the counseling, it has been found necessary to allow some occasional repetition, for which the reader's indulgence is requested. When any such separated portion is studied separately there is then less risk that an important point may be overlooked.

In formulating and expressing his ideas and insights about the healing of marriage the author is happy to acknowledge a very wide indebtedness.

He is indebted first to a large number of married couples who have allowed him the privilege of their confidence, and with whom he has looked at the many and varied difficulties and conflicts which have threatened their marriage and family life. From these distressed people more than from anyone else he has learned, and is still learning, most of his insights about the healing of marriage. But his ability to profit by such opportunities would have been seriously diminished if he had not been given much help by many first-class authorities in this field, some of whom merit special acknowledgment.

Professor David R. Mace has given constant inspiration and encouragement since 1952 through his personal friendship and the generous sharing of his deep experience by word and through his many writings. The National Marriage Guidance Council of Great Britain, with which the author enjoyed personal contact in 1952, has pioneered the "lay counselor" service and established the sound foundations and effective working methods on which similar work in many other countries, including Australia, has been based. To that body and to its secretary, A. Joseph Brayshaw, the author owes a continuing debt of gratitude.

He is also deeply indebted to the directors and administrators of many marriage counseling training centers in the United States of America for their generous personal friendship and help during his visits to them in 1958. In particular he would mention Dr. Karl Menninger of the Menninger Foundation, Topeka, Kansas; and Robert G. Foster, Ph.D.; and Dean Johnson, M.A., formerly of their Marriage Counseling Service. Also Emily Hartshorne Mudd, Ph.D., and her associates at the Marriage Council of Philadelphia; Aaron L. Rutledge and his associates at the Merrill Palmer School at Detroit; and Paul Popenoe and his associates at the American Institute of Family Relations at Los Angeles.

Nearer home, the author would acknowledge with continuing gratitude the fellowship and constant inspiration of his colleagues at the National Marriage Guidance Council of Australia since its formation in 1953, and at the Marriage Guidance Council of Victoria since 1949, together with the Marriage Councils of the other Australian States. In the constant struggle to keep the work going and to establish public confidence in it, the author and his colleagues have learned many useful things, and discussed many of the matters included in this book.

Finally, the author would pay a very sincere tribute of gratitude to his wife, who has taught him many practical things about marriage, and set an enduring pattern and standards of marriage which has made many of his efforts possible, and whose patience and forbearance in the author's work and in the typing of the manuscript of this book has involved considerable sacrifice. To her this book is most appropriately and affectionately dedicated.

CHAPTER I

What Is Marriage Counseling?

THE WORD "COUNSELING" is defined in many dictionaries as "giving advice" or "warning." People in trouble in their marital relationships have always been the recipients of all kinds of well-meant advice, and in that "educational" sense marriage counseling is probably as old and as universal as marriage itself. It has been carried on through the centuries and in many parts of the world by interested relatives and friends, and by ministers, doctors, teachers, lawyers and others with varying degrees of professional formality.

In previous centuries any marriage counseling had as its primary purpose the helping of wives to make the best of difficult situations in male-dominated "partnerships"; or possibly, in some cases, inducing husbands to be a little more understanding, sympathetic and tolerant to their wives and children. In such autocratic marriages wives were largely forced to make the best of whatever kind of marital situation they were drawn into, and marriage counseling was largely concerned with giving direct advice—or even using coercion. This attitude to marriage counseling still exists in some quarters.

But the steep rise in the divorce rate, and the large but unassessable separation rate over the last half century, suggest that these traditional methods of counseling are not sufficiently effective in the face of the strains of modern marriage. And this is amply confirmed by the experience of workers in many special fields of social service who come into direct or indirect contact with marital and family conflict. This has sometimes led to the belief that the situation is not open to remedy, that the relationship between husband and wife is too private and too personal to be accessible to any community welfare project.

In recent years, however—beginning in America in 1929, in Great Britain in 1938, and in Australia in 1947—there has been a gradual emergence and development of a new and much more rational approach to the whole project of helping people in serious marital and family conflict. This newer approach has been and is still being based on the practical experience of people of varying professional backgrounds, and it is being continually tested by trial and error experience rather than by theoretical ideas. It has borrowed from many basic disciplines, such as psychology, religion, medicine, sociology, education, psychiatry, and anthropology, and has been helped greatly by the technical resource of the tape recorder (in research institutes), through which interviews can be preserved with many of their emotional overtones, and from which many lessons can be learned.

The new approach differs from the older methods in many important respects.

In the first place it is conceived and carried out more as a therapeutic or healing than as an educational activity. It may, of course, still include some education; about, for example, the main principles underlying human relationships, and especially the most intimate relationships of marriage and parenthood.

This attempt at the healing of a "sick" marriage, like the healing of a sick person, rests on the conviction, confirmed more and more by experience, that the essential factor in all healing is a natural healing force with which the "healer" seeks always to cooperate.

It is found that the giving of advice, which is implied in the definitions of "counseling," does not generally achieve the desired end, however much the partners may be anxious for it. In almost every case the troubled partners will already have had a great deal of very "good," plausible, but often conflicting advice, which they have found to be either impossible to carry out, or ineffective when they have carried it out. Even then many of them come for counseling in the belief or hope that the "expert" will be able to hear what they have to say, and then give them better advice than any they have previously had.

On the other hand it has been abundantly confirmed that when a counselor can achieve with troubled people the kind of personal relationship in which they can progressively unburden their strained affronted and conflicting feelings, they then come to see themselves and their conflicts more clearly and objectively, and are in a much better position to make their own decisions about what they shall do. Marital disorders are practically always dominated by emotions, and emotions are "blinding" things, which distort people's judgment. Until people in the grip of intense and conflicting feelings can pour them out to someone who is willing to give them a full, genuine, attentive and accepting hearing, they will generally be unable to apply "sweet reason," either from their own thinking or from even the most "expert" advice.

The "sick" marriage can best be healed when the partners are helped to help themselves, when the counselor can sit down patiently with them and give them the chance to "see" themselves and their partners through the previously blinding mists of emotion, and then to apply "sweet reason" freed from the distortions of upset feelings, to their common task of rebuilding —or, if they see fit, dissolving—their partnership. Their decisions may be assisted by the offering of information when it is desired and seems appropriate, but the modern counselor feels very diffident about giving advice except in very special circumstances which will be discussed in later sections of this book.

A second difference from the older methods of marriage counseling is that modern counseling does not set out to interfere in people's marital troubles, nor does it indulge in coercion of any kind. Help is offered, but as in all healing it is more likely to be of value when it is sought and accepted by a willing "patient." Marriage counselors are not in any sense "managers" or "do-good-ers," and they will never "butt in," even when requested to do so by an anxious relative. They will offer their services, and then leave it to the people to decide whether or not they will accept them.

This fact, however, needs to be considered in relation to the growing conviction that the community has a definite stake in the success or failure of marriage, that marriage is a community as well as a private affair. To the extent that this is so the community has some responsibility to many people who are in great need of help, but who, for various reasons, are unwilling to seek counseling. There is a growing feeling in many communities that community organizations, such as the courts or possibly the Church, may have the public responsibility of putting judicial or moral pressure on some such couples to discuss their conflicts with a trained marriage counselor. Such discussions, although most appropriately conducted by a trained marriage counselor in a reasonably permissive atmosphere, are not quite the same as marriage counseling because the people come under external pressure. They are distinguished from counseling by being described as "conciliation." To conciliate is defined as "to gain, or win over; to gain the love or good will of such as have been indifferent or hostile; to pacify" (*Chambers's Twentieth Century Dictionary*, 1932).

When two people are persuaded to come for marriage conciliation, for example, by a divorce court judge, the first task of the counselor is to try to win their confidence—if possible to such a degree that they come to desire counseling. Then the conciliation gives place to counseling in its best sense. This winning of confidence of two previously unwilling or indifferent people requires more general skill, experience and patience, and other good qualities of personality than are even required for counseling.

A third difference between modern counseling and the older traditional methods is that the modern counselor does not feel competent or in any way disposed to judge either of the partners in conflict, or to impose his own moral values on them. He may ask them what they think the possible consequences of any attitude or action may be, and why they would want to do what they are doing, but in general the counselor sees his function as that of looking with each of them at the problem and the whole relationship, and accepting their feelings and their attitudes, and their conduct within the law. In this way their ultimate attitudes are dictated by their own consciences and by their views about the total situation.

Modern counseling then seeks to offer a service of such a nature that people are helped to help themselves; to provide an accepting relationship of a kind that will encourage each person to express his feelings in a permissive atmosphere, and progressively to achieve better insight into many aspects of the marital relationship. In this way each of them has the opportunity to make his own decisions as to what to do about it in an atmosphere of realism rather than of distorted emotion.

Such counseling has proved itself by far the best approach to people in marital conflict, as long as it is carried out by adequately trained people of suitable maturity and emotional stability. But it is not regarded as the only solution to marital problems. It is obvious that in this field as in others "prevention is better than cure," and modern marriage counseling is conceived as one important part of a comprehensive project for promotion of better marriage and family living. This project includes first-class universal comprehensive education and preparation for marriage and parenthood, which is so far in the earliest stages of its development, and also continuing research into marriage and family relationships, and into human relationships in general.

With this general background the question "What is marriage counseling?" might best be answered by giving a brief and rather summarized account of an actual case of a type sufficiently common to represent many cases which come to marriage counselors. Actually this case is built up from more than one, and is sufficiently disguised as to be unrecognizable.

The case is that of "John and Mary Smith," aged 28 and 32, married six years, with two children, four and two years old. Mary has come for help, and after settling in her chair she begins her story.

M. I'm worried and depressed about our marriage, I've tried everything I can think of to make things work out between us, and I've just about reached the end of my rope.

C. You're feeling pretty low. Would you like to talk about it?

M. Things were good for a time—until our first child was born. We both wanted children and looked forward to having them, but from the time Jimmy came, four years ago, John has been different. I managed to cope with the situation until Betty came two years ago, but from then on, when I needed his help and support more than ever, he's been unbearable. He's practically always moody and touchy, and he has begun to get into awful tempers over the slightest thing. I know I'm no angel, and I can take a fair amount of it, but now he has started to storm and rage at the children, even for absurdly trivial things, and they're getting terrified of him. Jimmy, the older one, is reacting with nightmares, which he didn't have before, and he gets asthma when the tensions are particularly bad.

c. It's the effect on the children that upsets you most?

M. Yes, that's the last straw, and it has made me feel that I must have some help. But even apart from that I've been concerned and even frightened about John. He has had some terrible rages recently and in one of them the other day he got an absolutely horrible look in his eyes, as if he might be going insane. He beat me about a month ago in one of his rages, and seemed sorry afterwards, but the old moodiness was back again within a few days. Something seems to be eating him, but I can't get any idea of what it can be. He won't talk things over, he either gets into a towering rage or just buries himself in his paper if I try.

c. You feel there must be something wrong with him and you're worried about what he'll do next?

M. I don't know about anything wrong with him, but something must be getting into him and making him like that. The house and garden are getting badly neglected now; he used to be very keen on the garden at least, but lately he doesn't seem to care. I'm wondering whether things are happening at his work too, he has generally been reasonably popular at the office, but Tom Clarke, one of his best friends, was asking me the other day whether his health has been all right apparently they had noticed him pretty moody and depressed there too. There must be something festering inside him, and he's too good a chap at heart to get like this. I still love him, but he seems to be doing all he can to kill my feelings for him. I can't understand what can be doing it, but I just wonder how much more I can stand.

C. You feel that basically he's good, but that something has got hold of him, and it's getting a bit close to the breaking point? Does he know you've come for help?

M. Oh yes, he knows about it. He thinks I need help more than he does, and he doesn't seem to think his conduct is bad enough to need help. He was happy for me to come, but I don't think he will be at all willing to come.

C. Would you mind if I wrote and invited him to come for a talk?

M. I'd be most grateful if you would, and I hope he will come.

This is a brief summary of the main parts of the first interview with Mary. Notice first how the counselor picked out the feelings that Mary was expressing, and responded to them rather than to the facts of her narrative, and with complete acceptance of them. Mary felt encouraged in this way to go on unburdening her feelings in a manner which she had not previously been able to do with anyone. Notice how, as she did so, she came to the expression of some more positive feelings, "He's too good a chap at heart to get like this. I still love him." No attempt was made in this first interview to turn Mary's thoughts to any possible way in which she might have been provoking John, and no attempt was made to find out any details of Mary's or John's background. Any such attempts might well have blocked the flow of feeling at this point, so they are kept for possible later attention.

The letter to John ran something like this:— "Dear Mr. Smith, Your wife has been to see me for help in the marital situation that has arisen between you. I think I could be of more help if I could have the opportunity of hearing how you feel about it. If you can manage to come for a talk I would be glad if you would make an appointment at some mutually suitable time. Yours faithfully, ——."

John came quite willingly in due course. He looked a normal enough person as he came in and began to tell his story.

J. I appreciated your direct invitation to come, and I must say Mary seems more relaxed since she came to you. I'm worried about the whole situation too, and I suppose I've put my foot in it pretty badly at times, but I'm fed to the teeth with Mary's attempts to dominate me, and to have everything her way. I've given up the attempt to make her realize that. Nothing I can say will ever convince her.

C. You feel you can't call your soul your own?

J. That's just about it. She was all right till the kids came, but since then I've been left out. All her attention goes to them, and the whole house has to revolve around them. She has worked out a rigid routine to the last detail, and nothing must ever interfere with it. She's always complaining of being overworked, but I'm sure she makes most of the difficulties for herself. The house is always in a mess in spite of the routine, and there isn't any comfort in it. It's not a home any more, and if I try to do anything to tidy it up it's always wrong. I never hear the end of it when she can't find something I might have put away. I'm not supposed to know anything about running a house.

C. Everything has to be sacrificed for the children, and you and the home mean nothing, whatever you try to do about it?

J. Yes, and it's not only in the house. I've got to work things at the office so that I never disturb the home

routine. If I'm home even twenty minutes late I have
to face a heavy cross examination about it. Even when
I'm home on time Mary demands to know everything
I've done, where I've been and who I've met, and I
object to that on principle. But it makes no difference,
and all I can do is to get behind the paper in self
defense. It would serve her right if I didn't come home
till later and stayed and had a drink with the boys. But
I don't want to make any more barriers between us if I
can help it.

c. You feel pretty fed up about it, but you're trying to
keep the relationship intact?

J. Yes, and I still have some glimmerings of hope that
things might be improved; that's why I'm here of course.
But after our previous efforts I can't say that I'm ter-
ribly optimistic. An uncle of Mary's, who seems to
think he's an expert in these matters, came to see us
some months ago, and gave me what he regarded as "a
good talking to." But he didn't seem interested in how
I felt about it, and in the end I told him that he didn't
know what he was talking about. But I suppose I can't
talk, because my mother had done much the same thing
to Mary a bit earlier, and that hadn't helped at all.

c. So you felt a bit skeptical about whether any outside
person could help you?

J. I'm afraid I did, but I realize they were both a bit prejudiced. But we had two really genuine efforts to find
a way through the trouble about a year ago without any
lasting result. We talked it out better than we've ever
been able to do since, and we agreed to let bygones be
bygones and to try to make a fresh start on a better
footing. But it looks as if Mary just can't help organizing
me and everything, and I can't bear being organized;
and the old tensions were on again within a few weeks.
So I felt I had some reason to be a bit despairing about

the prospects, until Mary decided to come to you. I must say I appreciate the way you've given me such a good hearing, but I can't see yet how it can help us to a better relationship.

c. You're still wondering how this sort of thing can help?

J. Yes, I'm afraid I am, but down deep I'm sure Mary is genuinely trying to work it out, and God knows I want to do it as long as I can keep some remnants of my personality. After all, we're both reasonable people and I love Mary more than I can say, even though I know she must sometimes have her doubts about it. And I think she still loves me, in spite of all the rows.

c. You feel pretty sure then that there are some basic reasons for hope. Enough to carry on in some more sessions, so that we can explore the situation a little more deeply?

J. Yes, that seems reasonable, and I feel better for having got all those things off my chest. Would you like me to make another appointment?

c. Mary is coming again early next week, so perhaps you could come a few days later, and tell me a bit more about yourself and how you feel.

In this summary of the first interview with John, notice again how the counselor has picked out the feelings from John's narrative, and shown acceptance of them. In this way he has gained John's confidence and made the deeper explorations which will be necessary in the future interviews much more straightforward. So far neither John nor Mary has shown much realization of their own destructive attitudes, nor has either of them been able to see much light about ways of improving their relationship. But with good rapport between the counselor and each of them, the necessary foundation has been laid.

It is clear from their attitudes that John and Mary are each at heart reasonable people, with sound personality structures, but that they are each unable to fulfil their roles adequately in marriage because of uncritical assumptions, habitual attitudes and emotional needs which have brought them into conflict. They have made efforts to overcome the conflicts, but these have been superficial, and have left the deeper factors unrealized and uncorrected. While this was the case they were doomed to failure.

As they were unable to see their own false attitudes any criticism would only put them still more on the defensive, and even the best advice would generally be futile, because neither would be able to carry it out while the false attitudes were uncorrected.

Here then are two good people, each hurt, bewildered and almost despairing, in deep and continuing conflict. Now that the children are beginning to feel all this—and are likely to be still more deeply affected—it is even more important that they should be helped to find their way through the distressing tangle. How can the stalemate be resolved? This may become clearer as we go on to look at the remaining interviews with John and Mary, beginning with the second interview with Mary.

After the usual kind of greeting the counselor asked Mary how she felt about the situation, to which Mary replied:

M. I don't know what you did to John the other day, but he has been a new man, much more relaxed and communicative, and I feel better too. But I still feel that there's an underlying tension, and it wouldn't take much to make it burst. I feel a bit as if I'm walking on a tightrope, and I'm trying to be very tactful.

C. Things are better, but you still have to watch your step?

M. How can we get past that kind of barrier, so that we don't have to hold ourselves in?

c. People who do this work find that it often helps to look at the backgrounds of those in trouble, to find out what they feel about the husband's and the wife's roles in marriage, and possibly why they feel as they do. Would you like to tell me something about yourself, and your earlier life?

M. I'm not quite sure what you would want, and it's not very interesting, but I'll try. I suppose the biggest thing that happened to me was that mother died suddenly when I was 16. I felt that the bottom had dropped out of my life, because she was the one person I had ever been able to lean on. You see Dad is a very good person, but he was never very strong, and my brother, he's two years younger than I am, has always been an irresponsible impulsive boy who had a passion for getting himself into trouble.

c. So you must have felt the loss of mother very keenly

M. Yes, and it wasn't improved by the fact that I had been all set to go to the University, but I felt I had to give that up and look after Dad and Harry, my brother. Mother had trained me pretty well in cooking, so I didn't find it too difficult, and Dad was most appreciative—he said several times that I had saved his life! He was very cooperative, and always came home punctually, but Harry was always difficult, he used to come home at all hours, and he was very careless and untidy. But I gradually got him trained so that at least I could run the home properly. If he came home late without telling me he had to get his own meal! He got into some pretty bad scrapes, and once I even had to go and bail him out when Dad was away.

c. You felt you had to train him pretty well so that you could run the home properly, but it was easier with Dad?

M. Well, if I was going to give up everything I'd wanted to do to look after them, I felt it was up to them to cooperate. But I got things well organized so that I could run the home well and also have some opportunity for some social life of my own. You see Dad's friends were all out of my age group, and Harry's friends didn't attract me one bit.

c. You felt a lot better when you got things organized?

m. Yes, I even managed to take a few university courses, but of course any full course would have been too much with my domestic responsibilities. But I felt I'd saved something out of the wreck, and I made some good friends. But with all I had to do I felt worried sometimes that I'd never get married. All my girl friends from school had gone off, and here was I, with a family of two helpless males and no husband.

c. You had all the responsibilities of motherhood without the pleasure and support of a husband?

m. That was just what I felt, but eventually of course I met John. He was the younger brother of one of my school friends. At first I didn't take to him at all, he was very much a "mother's boy." You see his father had walked out when he was about ten, and he and his sister were brought up by his mother and his grandmother. They just idolized him, and seem to have lavished everything on him. His mother still idolizes him and demands a lot of attention from him. Looking back now I realize that John never had to stand on his own feet, he got everything he wanted, and he often behaves now as if he believes he has a right to other people's love and cooperation.

c. You feel he never had to win the love and cooperation of people while he was growing up. Did he take much initiative in winning your love when he was courting you?

m. As I see it now I don't think he did. I'm afraid I rather took pity on him at the time he first showed real interest in me, and I really wasn't very hard to get. I felt that we clicked almost at once after he began to show interest, and I still felt that way till he started to get moody after Jimmy came. Then I felt he was demanding more attention than I could give him. He couldn't seem to understand how much the baby took my time and attention, and I couldn't neglect the baby.

c. Could it be that you were really mothering him at the beginning, and that he felt neglected when Jimmy came and needed your mothering?

M. I've sometimes wondered about that, and as we've been talking it seems to make sense. You know he's four years younger than I am.

c. And he'd been used to being mothered; while you'd been doing a lot of mothering to your father and brother?

M. It's extraordinary, now you mention it, how our two past histories interlocked with one another—how my satisfaction at mothering clicked with his need to be mothered—and how lost he must have felt when there were two helpless children to take all my mothering!

This second interview with Mary concluded with considerable growth in her understanding of John's difficulties, and the beginnings of better insight into her own attitudes. But so far she hasn't been able to see her own passion for organizing John, and the counselor has not made any attempt to confront her with it. It is found to be much more effective when people can come to achieve insight into their own destructive attitudes and to get some idea of why they have had them, than it is to attempt to confront them with such matters, at least at the beginning.

When the main emotional unburdening has been completed

and the rapport with the counselor is good it may be tempting for the counselor to say, for example, to Mary, "John feels that you are organizing him too much, and that's one thing that makes him sore." This is not likely to be very effective because Mary will probably be unable to see herself as others see her, and she will probably have rejected this idea already when John has tried to put it to her. A likely response to the counselor's effort at confronting her with it will be, "John's exaggerating this altogether; he has that stupid idea on the brain!" What can the counselor do then? Is he to argue it out with Mary and have the whole interview sidetracked into a conflict? Or is he to confront John later with the information that Mary doesn't agree with his ideas—which of course John knows already from his discussions with her? "Tale bearing" of this kind is not the function of the counselor, and it is apt to lead him into troubled waters.

If John and Mary each discuss the other's faults, and ignore their own (as seen by the other one) it is generally best, after the main emotional tensions have subsided to some extent, to arrange an interview with the two of them together—with mutual consent, of course. Then if, for example, John brings up Mary's excessive organizing, and Mary tries to discount it, John can answer her on the spot with particular examples. In this way the main points of conflict can be brought into the open and ultimately accepted by both of them, even if at this stage there is no apparent reconciliation.

After such a joint interview further sessions can be carried out with each alone, and an opportunity given for each to talk about the reasons and motives for these attitudes, so that better insight might be achieved. Further joint interviews can be arranged when there are any points of mutual concern to be clarified, and also later when any positive plans for the future are being considered.

If the first joint interview is held before the emotional tensions are partly relieved it might only serve to increase the tensions and inflict further wounds. Such interviews need be handled carefully, and if there seems to be undue heightening of tension it may be best to call a halt in the joint interview and to go on with individual interviews for a further period.

In the present case the growth of insight has so far been as good as one could expect, and the logical step is to have a second session with John, with the idea of learning how he sees his own background and that of Mary. This "two-dimensional" perception of backgrounds and of role perceptions in marriage is much more helpful than any "one-dimensional" perception, and it will make for much better clarification in further discussion with John and Mary.

The second interview with John began with a report of further relaxation of tension between them. It went on as follows:

c. You feel a bit more optimistic about it?

J. Yes, this is the best hope I've had because it seems to go deeper, but I still feel more organized than I like. But somehow Mary seems to be more generally approachable and even cordial. She told me she had a better understanding of how I've been feeling, since you and she got down to talking about how we grew up. I hadn't realized that would be of any great importance.

c. Would you like to tell me something about your own childhood as you see it?

J. Mary told you about Dad walking out, didn't she? But Mom did a magnificent job in bringing up my sister and me and holding down a job as well. Grannie was a great help and we all managed to get on well together. I've only seen Dad about twice since he left—he was a pretty hopeless alcoholic, and he was killed in a motor car accident a few years ago. I'm sure Mom was a lot better without him. She has still been a great help to me when I've felt pretty despairing, although she got Mary's back up. I still feel I owe her more than I can ever repay.

c. You still feel a pretty close relationship with your mother?

j. I've felt it more since things became difficult with Mary; and at about that time Mom had to give up her job and she needed more help from me.

c. I've noticed that Mary seems to be a maternal sort of person. Could it be that at the beginning she was giving you some good "mothering"?

j. I don't know about that—she was tremendously attentive and very loving, and she seemed to be able to anticipate most of my needs—that's what made it so difficult to understand after Jimmy came, when he seemed to take up a bit too much of her attention. I don't think that's good for any baby. But perhaps you could call it mothering—and after all she'd been pretty good at that sort of thing with her father and that stupid brother of hers—she still gets him out of an occasional scrape. I don't like it and I don't think he'll ever learn, and his father has never been able to do anything with him. Mary's father has always been a good natured chap, but he's weak and utterly ineffectual. Mary used to order him and her brother about till they could hardly call their souls their own.

c. Do you think that could have something to do with the way you felt Mary organized you; that she'd developed the habit of running the house that way, and got a real feeling of satisfaction out of it?"

j. Well, yes, I suppose that's why she does have such a passion for organizing. But I didn't notice it much in the early years of our marriage.

C. Could it be that you were getting such a lot of "mothering" attention at that time that you didn't notice the organizing?

J. And when I missed out on the attention because of the children I began to resent the organizing? I think I can see daylight there. But I still can't see any reason why I should put up with being managed. I'm not quite in the same category as her weak father and irresponsible brother. I don't want to be the big shot, but I *am* supposed to be the head of the house!

C. Do you thing that if you can stand on your own feet a bit more, and not be so dependent on what we've called the "mothering" or the attention, it may help Mary to ease up on the organizing?

J. Well, you know I've been doing that a bit since I came here last time—it's only a very short time—but I think I can make up my own mind what I ought to do in the house and the garden, and with the kids, and if Mary starts to disparage it I think I can let her think what she likes about it, without feeling so deeply insulted.

C. If she likes to think you're an incompetent fool you think you can let her think it without having to convince her immediately that you're nothing of the kind?

J. I don't know whether I could go quite that far yet, but I can see what you're driving at, and I'm determined to have a try at becoming less sensitive to her comments —if she goes on making them—and more steady on my own feet. You know I feel as if a big load has lifted from my shoulders, and I know what I've got to do, whatever Mary decides to do about it herself. And I've got a feeling that she's feeling a bit that way too.

Notice in these last interviews with Mary and with John how the counselor waited until there was a natural opening for his attempts at clarification of their feelings, and then how he set out to do it by asking questions, such as "Could it be that —?" rather than making dogmatic statements, such as "I think you feel that way because —." Dogmatic statements would be likely to stir up some opposition, and the counseling would then become sidetracked into a conflict between counselor and Mary or John. When it is put in the form of a question, Mary or John can easily say, "No, I don't think that's quite the way it is," and the counseling can then proceed to further elucidation without disruption.

As previously mentioned this was a fairly straightforward case, and John and Mary were capable of good insight. Also the account given has omitted some of the less applicable elements in the discussions and condensed the material into fewer interviews than would have actually happened. In many cases a great deal of patience is required on the part of the counselor before the two people come to achieve sufficient insight to be able to build a strong relationship. Sometimes one or both have such neurotic personalities that they can't do much without deeper individual psychotherapy. But this account may give some idea of what is being attempted in marriage counseling, and how a counselor sets out to do it.

John and Mary came together for an interview about ten days after the last session with John, and it was obvious that there was not much more to be done by the counselor. They were able to talk quite frankly about their new insights about themselves and their new understandings of each other, and to laugh good naturedly about John's choice of someone four years older than himself without realizing that he was looking for another "mother." And John could also point out that Mary, in choosing a man younger than herself, was gratifying her maternal feelings without altogether realizing it. The counselor asked Mary how she felt about the prospect of

John's asserting himself more, and Mary thought for a few moments, and then made the significant observation, "I think I can do with someone to depend on, and I hope he can do it. The children can do with a strong daddy too!"

It may be noticed that there was no discussion about the sex relationship in this case. This was mainly because neither John nor Mary referred to it at all, and because the counselor felt that they were growing so well in insight and in their relationship that there seemed no reason to ask about it. He was ready to follow their sequence of thought as they expressed themselves, and to accept whatever direction their feelings developed. By accepting their feelings and moving with them all the time the interviews were kept alive, and the two people were able to move forward to better and better understanding.

When this acceptance is not offered by the counselor there will often be long pauses in the interviews, and then it is easy for the counselor to begin "fishing," asking all kinds of questions unrelated to the train of thought. This is generally an expression of the counselor's anxiety, and it will devitalize the interview and tend to bewilder the people being interviewed.

Finally in the case of John and Mary it is easy to see why all the previous efforts of well meaning relatives, and the most genuine efforts of John and Mary themselves, were doomed to tragic failure. Until they could come to realize why each of them felt that way, and how much they were at the mercy of their uncritical assumptions and their unrecognized emotional needs, any attempt at reconciliation was sabotaged by the eruption of some of these hidden elements in the situation. By winning their confidence through giving each of them a full and attentive and accepting hearing, the counselor was then able to look with them at some of these unrecognized elements in such a way that they could face them and deal with them. That is the kind of approach that the marriage counselor makes. It has been fully confirmed that when people have been able to unburden themselves of their intense and conflicting feelings then, and only then, do they become able to "see," and to respond to "sweet reason."

This case record gives some confirmation to the growing feeling among workers in this field, that people are more likely to come to a more successful partnership by being helped to find their own way through their difficulties than by any direct advice from even the most "expert" counselor. There is certainly a place for directive advice, but it is found that the more experience any counselor has in marital or other kinds of counseling, the less prone he is to give advice, and the more effective his counseling becomes.

A good definition of marriage counseling is that given by Emily Hartshorne Mudd, M.S.W., Ph.D., Director of the Marriage Council of Philadelphia: "Marriage counseling is defined as the process whereby a professionally trained person assists two persons (engaged or marriage partners) to develop abilities in resolving, to some workable degree, the problems that trouble them in their interpersonal relationships as they move into marriage, live with it, or (in a small number of instances) move out of it. The focus of the counselor's approach is the relationship between the two people in the marriage rather than, as in psychiatric therapy, the reorganizing of the personality structure of the individual. The theoretical framework behind this approach presents the following hypothesis: If an individual can experience, during the counseling process, new ways of understanding of himself and his marriage partner and more satisfying ways of using himself in his daily relationships in marriage and with his family, he should be able to apply these acquired abilities to other problem situations as these arise in his daily living."[1]

As we shall see this definition may involve some clarification of the term "professionally trained person." In America the organized marriage counseling agencies are staffed by university graduates in one of several fields who have undertaken special training and gained experience in marriage counseling. In Great Britain, Australia, and some other countries much of the work is being carried out with acknowledged success by people without university degrees, who have however been very carefully "selected" and given what is tantamount to "professional training and experience." With this clarification the definition can be well applied to the work of marriage counseling everywhere.

The work of the marriage counselor touches that of the psychiatrist on one side, where it comes into contact with intra-personal disorders which may bring strains to the marital relationship; and that of the social worker on the other side, where it comes up against environmental strains on the relationship. It also comes into contact with the work of religious organizations in that many of the strains on the marital relationship have to do with religious attitudes. The more the marriage counselor can work together with each of these professions the better his work will be.

Before discussing the actual work of marriage counseling it would seem advisable to give some attention to the many interlocking contributory factors in marital disorder, and this will be the subject of the next chapter.

[1] "Man and Wife" edited by Emily Hartshorne Mudd, M.S.W., Ph.D. and Aaron Krich, Ed.D. W. W. Norton & Company, Inc., New York, 1957, p. 211.

CHAPTER II

Contributory Factors in
Marital Disorders

MARRIAGE HAS BEEN DESCRIBED as the most intimate, delicate and far-reaching relationship between people; and the family as a living, growing, and self-reproducing organism in a two-way relationship with the total environment: physical, cultural, social and spiritual. Human nature and human feelings being what they are there will inevitably be tensions and conflicts in marriage and family life. Successful marriage is not measured by the absence of conflict but by the ability of the partners to find constructive and rational ways of dealing with their conflicts, and growing to greater maturity and harmony together through these experiences.

When there is difficulty in dealing with marital conflicts to the extent that the marital relationship becomes progressively disturbed, it is inevitable that the results will extend beyond the two people involved. Apart from the effects of such disorder on the health, happiness and efficiency of the partners, which are important to society as well as to themselves, there will inevitably be adverse effects on the health and the development of the children, and these may soon become irreversible.

If marriage counselors and educators are to be of adequate

help to people in marital conflict it is necessary for them to have some over-all concepts of the many inter-related contributory factors in marital disorders, so that they can have some familiarity with the terrain into which they are likely to be led.

For clarity of description it is helpful to think of the most common contributory factors under three headings, the intrapersonal, the inter-personal, and the environmental. The intrapersonal factors will include those which are concerned with the personalities of the two partners and their fitness in various ways for the stresses and strains of marriage and family life. The inter-personal factors are concerned with the living dynamic relationships between them, and their ways of dealing with tensions and conflicts. The environmental factors are concerned with the influence of the physical, cultural, social and spiritual realities—and unrealities—which bear on the two partners and on their marriage and their family life.

It is quite obvious that defects within the personalities of one or both of the partners will bring about disturbances in their relationships and also in their environment. Disturbances in their relationships will also have some effect, sometimes a profound effect, on their inner personalities and on their environment. And environmental pressures may be serious enough to disturb both their inner personalities and their relationships.

It is generally unnecessary for the counselor to disentangle the relative influences of these three sets of factors to any detail—indeed, it would generally be impossible to do so in any case. But if he is aware of the general nature and extent of these three groups of factors and of the kind of influences they can exert on marriage and family living, he is less likely to overlook or disregard them when seeking to understand the feelings and attitudes of the people who come for his help.

1. SOME INTRA-PERSONAL FACTORS WHICH CAN CONTRIBUTE TO MARITAL DISORDER

One of the most significant facts about modern marriage and the disorders which may emerge in it is that with a few exceptions which hardly ever apply, people over 21 who are unmarried or whose marriage has been legally terminated are free to marry without any safeguards regarding their fitness or suitability for marriage. People under 21 and above a minimum age generally laid down by the law of their country can also marry under these conditions with no safeguard beyond the consent of their parents (which is often obtained under heavy pressure).

Once they are married, however, the doors shut and the exit is barred, even if they find to their mutual disillusionment that they have made a stupid mistake and have come to detest each other. It is of course essential that society should take all possible steps to safeguard its own stability without too much interference with the liberty of its members, and the only practical way to reconcile these two essentials would seem to be the fullest and most adequate preparation for marriage as a universal requirement.

The laws of any country concerning divorce, annulment and judicial separation are admittedly imperfect attempts to do what is basically impossible: to control human attitudes and human behavior by legislation. But every society has found it necessary to put such legal restraints on the dissolution of marriage because the community has an essential stake in its preservation wherever that is possible, and the courts are continually on the lookout for attempts to evade the law by mutual arrangement and the faking of evidence.

The result of this freedom to marry without any necessary safeguards as to personal fitness is that many serious marital disorders are primarily caused by the personal unfitness of one or both partners for marriage. Fortunately this in many cases is not beyond repair, and it is therefore important for all who seek to help those in marital trouble to be aware of the different kinds of unfitness and of ways by which they can possibly be helped. Some of the most common of them will therefore be discussed.

a. *Ignorance or misinformation.* With more widespread projects concerned with education for marriage there is probably a steady lessening of ignorance and misinformation. But it is still true in most if not all countries that a large proportion of people who marry do so with the vaguest and often the most distorted ideas about such important matters as the sexual impulses in men and women, the meaning of love, the expression of love in the sexual relationship, the principles of personal relationships, and even about such "practical" matters as home management, cooking, sewing, carpentry, first aid and home nursing. Matters concerning parenthood and child management also have much to do with the general conduct of marriage, and can be suitably dealt with in the early years of marriage, if possible before the children come.

Everyone who marries has received a great deal of information of a kind, but in all too many cases it will have come from sources which are grossly inadequate and often completely misleading, such as the general conversation of their friends, neighbors, colleagues, and, strangely less often, of their parents. This is supplemented by the subtle influences of the mass media, popular novels, "soap opera" on radio and television, and the movies, not to mention the seductive practices in mass advertising. Even many apparently sophisticated and knowing people are found to have some very distorted ideas about some of the essential facts of life and of human relationships, so it has generally been found wise to take nobody for granted in this field.

In addition to correct information about the essential facts relating to sex, love, marriage, home making and parenthood, some training in self-control and in constructive attitudes to these things is essential. It has been found that merely giving information about such matters as sex may only make it more possible for undisciplined people to participate in all kinds of distorted and even abnormal sexual practices. Sex is an energy which needs harnessing and direction as well as knowledge, and this aspect of education for marriage will be dealt with in the next section ("Immaturity") as will other distorted attitudes.

This difficulty of lack of correct information and knowledge is of course best dealt with by education from earliest childhood onwards, and particularly in a comprehensive premarital preparation, often with groups of young people, and with encouragement of free discussion under wise and understanding leadership. But when it is discovered during counseling in marital disorders that there is considerable ignorance or misinformation about essential matters the counselor must be able to give the necessary information in a simple, natural and reverent manner, and in some cases to put the partners in touch with other sources of information, such as other counselors, or suitable books. But no book will take the place of the personal relationship between counselor and the partners for the passing on of information in the necessary atmosphere of good personal rapport. Part of the training of a marriage counselor is therefore concerned with knowledge of these things, healthy attitudes to them, and ability to communicate them to people in an effective manner.

b. *Immaturity* is probably the background factor in most marital disorders, even when the presenting problem seems to be of some other kind. Marriage is meant to be a partnership between adults, and adulthood is not mainly a chronological matter, even though the law finds it necessary to regard people over 21 as adults. In general the personality of the immature person is basically sound, but untrained and undisciplined. This may bring about very intense strains and conflicts in marriage because the give and take and the responsibilities are too great for the undeveloped personality to cope with reasonably.

But as with ignorance, it is often quite possible to help people to overcome this personality deficiency. Considerable time and patience are required, but if the marriage can be held together for the necessary time and the people given enough encouragement and help, the marriage relationship itself can be a very maturing experience. Everyone has had the pleasure of watching quite immature youngsters growing and developing in maturity to a remarkable extent through the stimulus of marriage and parenthood.

Many immature people find it more difficult to develop because their immaturity is combined with some degree of neurotic personality structure that makes them unreasonably demanding, unreasonably anxious, dependent or obsessional. This will be dealt with in a later section of these intra-personal factors.

Immaturity, with or without obvious neurotic trends in the personality, may well cause serious marital disorder because it may have led to hasty or unwise choice of mate. The marriage would then have begun under a great handicap. Even from the point of view of chronological age the qualities which attract a boy or girl at, say, 23 are often very different from those which attract at, say, 18; and it is what attracts at 23 that is more important for continuing marriage. This is not to suggest that people should not marry under 21, but that such early marriages may provide more and deeper challenges to people.

Another common effect of immaturity which may bear heavily on marriage is that either partner or both may have failed to cut loose from emotional dependence on their parents when they are still financially dependent on the parents, or have been so for a long time. In such cases of emotional dependence the parents themselves will often be unduly involved in any marital conflict between the young people, because they feel unable to stand by while their son or daughter is unhappy or in any marital difficulty. In many such cases the entry of parents into the situation, however well-meant and even necessary, may make the conflicts still more intense and less open to reconciliation.

Most of these situations will be helped much more by a trained marriage counselor who is not emotionally involved in the situation than by any parent or close friend. When they come to the marriage counselor the situation often demands great tact and patience, and considerable emotional stability in the counselor—particularly when he has to handle hostile and interfering relatives as well as the two young people in conflict. It helps greatly if he can win the trust and the cooperation of the worried parents, which he has to do without disclosing the confidential material given to him by the partners. Then he might be able to induce the parents to keep their hands off the situation so that he has a more straightforward opportunity with the partners.

Immaturity may be general, involving all aspects of the personality, or it may be limited to one or more aspects. For purposes of discussion it is useful to think of it from each point of view separately.

Physical immaturity, or lack of physical development, is generally fairly obvious, and will have been in most cases the subject of medical treatment. It is not often a factor in marital discord, and if it seems to be present it is appropriately referred to a doctor for help.

Intellectual immaturity may show itself as ignorance, rigidity of thought and ideas, or as plain stupidity. In these days it is possible to make some assessment in any doubtful cases by having various intelligence tests carried out. Here again this kind of immaturity may not have very profound effects on marriage unless there is gross inequality in intelligence. Many quite unintelligent people manage to get on well in marriage and even parenthood if they are generally good-natured, because they tend to demand much less than more intelligent people from marriage.

Vocational immaturity may show itself by a lack of capability for a reasonable job, either the running of a home on the part of a woman or the carrying out of a "breadwinning" job on the part of the man. Either of these may well bring strains on the marriage, and sometimes this situation can be relieved to some extent if the person or persons concerned are willing to accept reasonable training in the particular field.

Emotional immaturity is a very common intra-personal factor in one or both partners concerned in a marital disorder, and some aspects of it have already been mentioned, such as failure in emotional emancipation from parents, and impulsive or unwise choice of mate. Emotional immaturity may show itself in many different ways.

A fairly common manifestation is in the sexual attitudes and relationships. In the extreme case homosexuality is likely to cause physical and emotional unfitness for marriage. In the majority of cases homosexuality is regarded as being an acquired rather than a constitutional disorder, and most of the openly homosexual men and women have no desire to marry. But a number of less marked cases of homosexuality are first induced to seek help after marriage when the sexual relationship has been found to be inadequate or quite hopeless.

In addition to these, emotional immaturity may show up in

less definite form in what is termed "latent homosexuality." Every man and woman has some of the chemical and emotional attributes of the opposite sex. In the vigorously "masculine" man and the graciously "feminine" woman, these opposite qualities are not sufficiently marked to cause any disturbance. But sometimes an apparently normal heterosexual man or woman may have sufficient of the opposite qualities to bring about disorders in the sexual and the personal relationships of marriage. Many cases of impotence or partial impotence in men may be explained in this way, and some cases of frigidity in women. Others may be more fittingly regarded as due to some form of neurotic illness, but this is a matter for psychiatric appraisal.

Homosexuality, actual and latent, is regarded by Edmund Bergler, M.D. as primarily fear of the opposite sex rather than primarily attraction to persons of the same sex. If this be true, the attraction to people of the same sex may be caused or intensified by a deep need for companionship and intimacy, which after all is something which all normal people tend to have. It is possible that many cases in which husbands and wives find it difficult to be socially at ease with persons of the opposite sex, and even more when they feel the urge to congregate almost exclusively with members of their own sex, may have their roots in this form of emotional immaturity. The common social practice of men and women remaining in separate groups throughout the evening at a party may be a very mild example of this tendency. Some cases in which husbands for quite plausible reasons devote themselves to "all male" pursuits to the real neglect of their wives and families, or in which wives overdo it with "all female" projects to the neglect of their domestic obligations, may also be indications of this kind of emotional immaturity.

Many of these milder varieties of immaturity will not require

—and the people will generally not be willing to undergo—any special medical or psychiatric treatment. If they are willing to face their difficulties and set out to develop their sociability to a more mature level, the marriage relationships will tend to improve to a more satisfactory state.

But when the difficulties are more serious and destructive to the marital harmony it may be necessary for the marriage counselor to refer one or both partners for some form of psychotherapy.

A second group of manifestations of emotional immaturity is in abnormal dependency. This is often seen as a kind of social timidity and shyness and a feeling of inadequacy and personal inferiority. Such people are often emotionally dependent on one or both parents, whose need to feel needed may well cause them to remain rather over-possessive. When they are away from home, even for a short time, they may feel a great lack of confidence and a need for someone on whom they can lean.

When two such young people meet, their emotional needs may encourage a very deep bond of sympathy between them, and a feeling of mutual confidence when they are together. If they are of the same sex this may intensify any homosexual trends, and if of the opposite sex it may well seem to them as "falling in love" and lead on to marriage. But it soon becomes obvious that each is trying to use the other for reassurance and support, and neither has the qualities to supply those needs in the other through the humdrum everyday concerns and the ups and downs of marriage. It was easy enough when they only saw each other outside their homes and all dressed up and on their best behavior, but marriage may well bring mutual disillusionment and recrimination, and even the possibility that one or both may be attracted to someone else who again may appear to satisfy the dependency needs.

This kind of situation may often be recognized by a good pre-marital counselor, because of small indications in either of them of possessiveness, sulkiness when demands are not fully met, and general "spoiled child" behavior. This would suggest that much of the "love" into which they have fallen is really self-love, and not what they think it to be. It may be very difficult or even impossible for the two young people, so deeply "in love," to see anything of this, and the counselor's most helpful contribution might then be to try to keep their mutual confidence in him, so that the way might be open for him to help them when the almost inevitable troubles come.

When the disillusionments and recriminations begin after marriage the emotional conflicts may become very intense, and there may be deep wounds on both sides, even leading to a "nervous breakdown" in one of them. In our society, in which the husband is generally the breadwinner, emotional immaturity is generally more destructive to marriage when it occurs in men than in women. Two common situations of this kind may be described.

In the first case Mary may find after marriage, to her increasing anxiety and despair, that she only has about one quarter of John's loyalty and companionship, the rest being held grimly and determinedly by John's mother, who "never approved of Mary anyhow," and has so over-mothered John that he has never been able to cut himself loose from her apron-strings. Now he can't decide anything without asking his mother's opinion, and he accepts it and acts on it irrespective of Mary's ideas or indeed of the true interests of their home and family. His mother has only to make a skillfully vague implication of her "disappointment" at John's "ingratitude," with the spoken or unspoken climax, "after all I've done for you," and he is clay in her hands. If John is ever induced to do anything of which his mother might disapprove he may not even be able to tell her, "for fear it might upset her."

In the second case it soon transpires that in the home John must get everything he wants, and when he wants it, or there's trouble. If a meal is a few minutes late, or the toast is slightly burned, or the egg slightly overcooked, he gets angry even to the point of losing his temper. He expects Mary to be at his beck and call in everything, as his overattentive mother used to be, and when she doesn't fulfill these insatiable demands he gets into a sulky or angry mood and accuses her of not loving him any more. At the same time he has given up all the little attentions and gestures of "love" which he used to offer before their marriage, and he doesn't feel any responsibility to help Mary in any of her domestic activities, even when she is ill or tired. Mary may then have to face the extraordinary inconsistency of a husband who is a charming fellow to everyone outside the home, and a touchy, moody, demanding "spoiled child" in the home, who constantly indulges in temper tantrums and even physical violence when his demands are not fulfilled. She finds it impossible to understand, and her desperate efforts to cope with the emotional scenes only seem to make things worse.

This kind of situation occurs among otherwise good, generous, conscientious people. John's mother would probably be astounded at any suggestion that she had over-mothered him. She, like many middle-aged mothers, may have ached to feel needed, and found little emotional inspiration from her own husband. She would then have unwittingly used her son to fill the aching emotional void, and failed to see that as he grew up he couldn't continue to need her in quite the same way. So instead of turning her attention outward to some kind of social service in which she could continue to feel needed, she kept her claws fastened on John, who always had been affectionate to her and ready to do what she wanted.

The same kind of situation of course can happen with an overdependent, demanding wife, who will never let her husband out of her grasp, and who turns on a temper tantrum whenever he goes against her demands in any way. Such a wife may well team up with her mother against her husband, who will feel very much "odd man out" or even the "villain" of the piece.

This demanding attitude may often express itself in demands for frequent sexual intercourse by the husband at all kinds of times of day or night, irrespective of his wife's feelings or doings. This ignores the fact that love, of which intercourse is a deep symbol, is not properly something one can have on demand, but rather something one seeks to win from one's partner. It may also express itself in the opposite kind of demand from the wife, that her husband must never have any sexual relations with her. The "spoiled child" of either sex will show this character in any aspect of personal relationships, including sex.

In some cases the marital disorder is triggered off by a change in one of the partners some years after the wedding. It may be that a demanding husband finds a wife whose dependency is expressed by willingly allowing him to dominate her. Then for some reason, possibly after the children come and she becomes more mature, or possibly because his demands become unbearable, she begins to stand firm on her own autonomy, and to resist his domination. It may be very difficult for such a husband to adapt himself to this change in the relationship, and it may need the skillful and patient help of a good marriage counselor to keep the marriage from breaking up if the husband fails to see and accept what is happening.

A somewhat similar difficulty may happen when, some years

after the wedding, the husband begins to grow to maturity much more rapidly than his wife. This may happen because of promotion in his job, with much greater challenges to him, the association with more mature people, and possibly travel in connection with his work. In such cases it may be very difficult for his wife to "keep up" with him, and it may demand more tact than he possesses to avoid making her feel inferior and inadequate. Here again the frank facing of such a situation and a genuine sustained attempt by both of them to meet it, possibly with the help of a good counselor, may well help his wife to rise to the challenge and develop many latent qualities of great value.

Another form of immaturity may be described as spiritual immaturity, and it may also show itself in various ways. There may be a kind of spiritual overdependency, which looks on God as a kind of over-indulgent "father figure," and prayer as a sort of spiritual Aladdin's lamp. This kind of attitude may get by while things are going well, but it will not sustain anyone in times of great strain and trouble because it is unreal. If it is present in a husband it may encourage him to be quite irresponsible and to take no thought at all for the morrow instead of the "no anxious thought" suggested in the Sermon on the Mount. The more mature spiritual attitude is surely what has been described as "the higher carelessness," doing all that one can, with all the help available, and then being content to leave the results—or apparent lack of result—in the "better hand than ours."

In addition to this "magic and superstition" kind of spiritual immaturity, there is often a kind that shows itself in very rigid spiritual attitudes, which tries to insulate those who have it from "the world, the flesh and the devil," and to keep them in an ivory tower of exclusiveness, completely out of harmony with the Founder of Christianity, who could dine with publicans and sinners, and deliberately make His way among all kinds of people. The most common difficulty that such attitudes produce in marriage is that many such rigid people are not content to apply their ideas to their own lives (which of course they have every right to do if they see fit), but also try to impose them upon other people, particularly upon their marriage partners, and upon the children, irrespective of the feelings of the others.

Some difficulties of this kind are brought about when, some time after marriage, one of the partners undergoes a "conversion" to a rigid religious sect; and in tremendous religious zeal, and considerable blindness to the implications of what he is doing, makes it his most important life-work to "convert" his partner and the family. The inner blindness is generally so great, and the inner conviction so strong, that even the most skillful and patient counseling may find no point of entry into his rigid formulations. The other partner may well be helped to carry on with patience and tolerance, quietly standing firm on her own convictions and being willing to "agree to differ."

There seems to be a rich field of specialized counseling on this spiritual level, so that marriage counselors can have some really competent spiritually equipped authorities to whom they may refer people with such problems, if they are willing to be referred. But this is by no means likely to happen in the rigid cases, and those in which an unreal religion happens to act as the opium of spiritually immature people.

Before leaving the subject of immaturity as an intra-personal factor in marital disorders it is well to remind ourselves that many of the ostensible causes of marital conflict are really outward manifestations of immaturity. Some of these may be considered at this point.

Intemperance in one form or another is a very common apparent cause of marital breakdown. Repeated drunkenness has been put forward as one of the most common of all causes by people who are mainly concerned with the more obvious destructive factors without looking far beneath the surface to deeper causes. Here again the boundary line between emotional immaturity and neurotic illness as a cause of alcoholism is vague and ill defined, and it is more of academic interest to the marriage counselor, because it is outside his province to attempt the cure of such intra-personal disorders. When it becomes a serious threat to a marriage, or indeed to any person's health or general welfare, it is properly the concern of such professional help as given by psychiatrists, often helped by a period of institutional care and discipline, and such "mutual help" organizations as Alcoholics Anonymous. It may be the counselor's task, when such troubles come to him in his marriage counseling, to try to persuade the alcoholic to submit himself for proper treatment, and to see the value and the possibility of relief.

The alcoholic may provide a very difficult problem in marriage counseling because he seldom has any idea of how his conduct appears to other people, and he may be so much at the mercy of his addiction that even with all the misery of "hangovers" he still has little motivation to undergo the difficult discipline involved in overcoming it. He seems to have little recognition of the suffering and distress imposed on his partner and of the intensity of his demands in many cases for sexual intercouse at the very time when his wife is likely to feel nauseated by his crude uncouth behavior. Beyond all of this there is often a further problem in the excessive spending of money on his alcoholic excesses, and in the growing neglect of his home and surroundings and the progressive loss of the respect of his growing children, even if by some good fortune he is able to keep a reasonable job.

Another form of intemperance which may have quite devastating effects on marriage is in the spending of money, particularly in response to what may be termed the gambling fever. When this gets hold of any man or woman it may bring the partnership to financial ruin unless some strong measures can be taken to restrain the spending, and unless some good psychotherapy can bring the underlying immaturity or neurotic trends to the surface so that they can be dealt with decisively. Here again such difficulties are generally best referred by the marriage counselor for appropriate psychotherapy, without which any apparent recovery is likely to be temporary.

The overspending of *time* may also be destructive to marriage. For example, one of the partners may become so addicted to some craze that his home and even his job are neglected, not to mention his personality. Almost any activity can become the object of overaddiction, even religious activities, and these addictions are also indications of either emotional immaturity or of definite emotional or mental disorder. They are seldom helped greatly by exhortation, but are more appropriately regarded as symptoms of deeper disorder which is best dealt with by psychotherapy.

Irresponsibility is also frequently suggested as a cause of marital disorder, but here again it is probably better regarded from the point of view of treatment as an outward and visible sign of immaturity. It is more within the field of counseling than the various forms of intemperance except when it is a symptom of deeper emotional disorder, such as the psychopathic personality, which will be referred to in due course. Some cases of irresponsibility can be helped over a period of time by the marriage partner, through repeated exposure of the irresponsible person to situations which demand responsibility, taking the risk of evasion of the challenge and being ready to accept some inconvenience when that happens.

c. *Illness, physical and mental,* may sometimes be found as a decisive intra-personal causative factor in marital disorder.

The heavy burden of severe or repeated physical illness, possibly including hospitalization and surgical operations, may overwhelm married couples who have not the physical, emotional and possibly the financial stability necessary to cope with it. When it happens early in a marriage it might be particularly difficult for them to negotiate. In some cases the help of social workers and of good neighbors and relatives will have a decisive effect on the preservation of the marriage.

A less obvious kind of physical illness fairly common in these days, and often a source of strain to a marriage is exhaustion from overwork, particularly in the case of young mothers with demanding children and insufficient help. They often become deeply disillusioned by the never-ending daily grind, so different from their rosy dreams about marriage and parenthood. They are too tired to be of much inspiration to their husbands when they come home tired after a trying day to an untidy house, a late meal, crabby children and a miserable wife. Tempers tend to be much more easily provoked, and the two partners may easily find themselves drawing further and further apart. There may also be financial worries to add to the trouble.

These situations need counseling to allow each of the partners the opportunity of unburdening disturbed and hostile feelings and apprehensions and worries. Sometimes this is enough to enable them to take hold again, with the help of relatives and friends. Sometimes they need help towards more efficient household management and better use of available financial resources. In such troubles as these marriage counselors need to have an awareness of the social welfare resources that may be available and appropriate to the situation.

The most common mental illness met with in the background of marital disorders is what is called psychoneurosis, or neurosis for short. The marriage counselor does not set out to treat neurotic illness, but he must be able to recognize some of the indications of such disorders, so that he is less likely to waste time and effort in trying to reason people out of them, or to make them worse by misunderstanding. He is then more confidently able to refer them if necessary for medical treatment.

How can they be recognized? A simple description has been offered by Albert Ellis, M.A., Ph.D. in his book "How to Live with a Neurotic" (Crown Publishers, Inc., New York, N. Y.). "Psychologists usually label as 'neurotic' only those individuals who are so inappropriate in their feelings and so ineffective and disruptive in their behavior that they sooner or later get into rather serious difficulties of their own making."

The inappropriateness of feeling may be shown in undue anxiety, irrational fears (such as claustrophobia), crippling indecision even about straightforward matters, extreme touchiness and hostility over trivial things, seeing "insults" in perfectly natural attitudes, and suspicion of even the most genuine motives. In other cases there may be obsessional feelings, compulsive striving for perfection and rigid demands on others for perfection, blaming them bitterly when they fail to meet expectations. There may also be extreme or morbid guilt feelings.

These inappropriate feelings generally extend beyond the domestic relationships to every other relationship. There are frequent conflicts in the person's job, in which everyone else is wrong and he is the "injured party." This expression of inappropriateness in a wider field may help to differentiate neurotic illness from the emotional immaturity already considered, but there is no clear point of division between the two.

The neurotic is constantly "ridden" rather than in control of his life, he is compulsive, self-centered and demanding, even demanding love and friendship at the same time he is doing everything possible to alienate those who would help him. When it suits him he can turn on the charm, but this is superficial and short lived, and turns quickly to hostility when his desires are not fulfilled. He may have the capacity to succeed but stands all the time in his own light, making the most plausible excuses, and many obviously stupid ones, for his failures.

The important feature about all of these inappropriate feelings and attitudes and the ineffective and disruptive behavior is that they are not open to "reason" or to the direct awareness or control of the neurotic or of anyone else. They can only be tackled by helping the person to work backward from them so as to discover the false concepts and assumptions about life and about people, including himself, which are behind the symptoms; for example that other people "must" fulfil any person's arbitrary expectations, or that love is something that can be obtained or preserved at "pistol point." There are many such false assumptions about life and they are extremely varied, and well protected by very strong psychic defenses. That is one reason why psychotherapy is such a skilled, patient and complex art.

It is easy to see how such intense and falsely based feelings can be so destructive to the marriage relationship, and how all attempts at "sweet reason," criticism, advice and admonition will be doomed to failure. Unless the neurotic is willing to face the "blood, toil, tears and sweat" of possibly prolonged psychotherapy (which means accepting his need for help), the trouble tends to recur.

An interesting and important aspect of neurosis in marriage is that people often make their choice of a mate in a manner greatly influenced by their neurotic needs. For example an insecure boy who has a neurotic need to get girls to "fall" for him might come to marry a girl with a sense of inferiority who needs a "masterful" boy. When the neuroses of the two partners "neutralize" each other the marriage might well be very satisfactory to both of them. When the relationship is or becomes satisfactory it may be quite harmful to the marriage to set out to treat the neurosis of one of them, because the whole balance of the marriage may be completely upset. It is often better in such cases to "let sleeping dogs lie."

Another type of mental abnormality which can be very destructive to the marriage relationship is what is called the psychopathic personality. This term covers a number of different kinds of disorder seen primarily in the field of behavior. While the neurotic feels a significant part of the trouble within himself, however much upset his trouble may bring about for other people, the psychopath usually shows little signs of disturbed inner feelings, and practically the whole disturbance is felt by other people.

In many ways the behavior and relationships of the psychopath are comparable with those of the grossly immature, and this is in harmony with certain physical characteristics of the psychopath. The tracings generally found in electroencephalograms of psychopathic persons are often similar to those found in children, and the conformation of the capillary loops in the nail bed of their fingers is also frequently like that found in children.

"These people" wrote David Stafford-Clark ("Psychiatry Today" Penguin Books, 1952) "are impulsive, feckless, unwilling to accept the results of experience and unable to profit by them, sometimes prodigal of effort but utterly lacking in persistence, plausible but insincere, demanding but indifferent to appeals, dependable only in their constant unreliability, faithful only to infidelity, rootless, unstable, rebellious, and unhappy. A survey of their lives will reveal an endless succession of jobs, few of which have been held for more than six months, many of which have been abandoned after a few days; very little love but often a great number of adventures, very little happiness despite a ruthless and determined pursuit of immediate gratification."

It is easy to see how unfit such people are for the responsibilities and obligations of marriage and parenthood, and there is no doubt that they are responsible for a great deal of misery, bewilderment and despair in their marriages. It is extraordinary how much they are trusted in spite of many failures, and how often their plausibility and even charm (when it suits them) get them (temporarily) out of trouble. But their lack of apparent insight, their unwillingness to undergo any kind of psychotherapy, and the futility of most efforts to help them to better social responsibility, make the outlook generally far from promising. In most cases of any severity the marriage either breaks up or else the other partner makes the best of an intensely difficult situation with whatever safeguards can be established. In some cases it is found after a period of strain and conflict, and possibly great financial loss, that the person has made a bigamous marriage without giving any hint of the existence of a previous wife and family.

The most important consideration relating to the psychopathic personality as it affects marriage is the discovery of the disorder before marriage, which would generally be during pre-marital counseling. It is possible that very much unhappiness in marriage would be prevented if more people understood something of the indications of this abnormality and of the difficulty of changing the character of such people. This might involve considerable knowledge of the past activities of prospective marital partners, and this is much more difficult in these days when so many people choose their partners from outside their own neighborhood, and therefore may know much less about their backgrounds. The choice of a life partner is surely important enough to warrant a fairly full knowledge, rather than a series of unsupported "assurances," or a very short acquaintance of a fairly superficial kind.

The third group of mental disorders which may render

people unfit for the responsibilities and obligations of marriage and parenthood includes what are called the psychotic illnesses, or in more popular terms the insanities. The occurrence of a psychotic illness does not necessarily bring about a hopeless marital situation, any more than a severe physical illness will do. Treatment of many people with such illnesses is much more successful in these days, and many of them are very responsive to the devoted care of an understanding partner and relatives.

The psychotic may generally be distinguished from the neurotic, although there is no sharp line of demarcation, by the fact that he lacks insight into reality as well as into his own inner attitudes, while the neurotic, with defective insight into himself, generally has reasonable insight into the realities of life. Because of his lack of insight into reality the psychotic shows more irrational attitudes, and is much less "accessible" to counseling and psychotherapy than the neurotic.

The commonest types of psychotic illness are the "affective disorders" which mainly but not entirely involve feelings, and the various forms of schizophrenia, in which feeling, thinking and behavior are generally all involved in the disorder.

The affective psychoses are more common in the second half of life, and are of two general types, which in some cases alternate with one another in the same person. First are the depressive illnesses often termed "melancholia," characterized by progressive inconsolable sadness and by deadness of feeling and utter pessimism. There may be strong delusions of guilt and failure, and about bodily functions. The other type includes the elated-feeling people, with bouts of tireless energy and enthusiasm and increasing restlessness, in which everyone is expected to share.

The melancholic people may bring some strains on marriage, but with reasonable understanding, which avoids attempts to argue them out of their depressions and delusions, they are generally manageable except for certain agitated types that need some restraint. There is often some danger of suicide, and such people are usually hospitalized and given special treatment, which is reasonably successful in many cases.

People suffering from mania may need urgent restraint in some cases, and particularly some protective measures against overenthusiastic spending of money, which may rapidly reduce a family to financial straits. They are usually responsive to treatment in hospital, and may remain well for some time until a further attack of mania or a gradual drift into a period of melancholia.

Schizophrenia in its various forms is commonest in the first half of life, although one form, the paranoid or delusional, often occurs in older people, either as a gradual development from the earlier form or as an apparently fresh illness. The most common early indications of schizophrenia are indifference, incongruity of emotions, such as giggling in the face of tragedy, irresponsibility and lack of initiative, dreaminess, and emotional withdrawal. There may be bizarre associations of ideas, delusions and hallucinations, and in one form fixed symbolic posturing. In early stages a young person may become involved in an impulsive marriage, and with the strains and responsibilities of marriage, and particularly those of pregnancy and childbirth, may suffer a serious breakdown in health and sanity.

The most difficult "psychotic" marital problem is probably that of what is called "paranoid schizophrenia," a chronic disorder characterized by fixed delusions, which are woven into the person's total attitudes and are completely resistant to any kind of argument or persuasion. They may sound completely plausible at the beginning, and often cause very great embarrassment, inconvenience and distress to many people, and particularly to the marriage partner.

A common delusion affecting the marriage relationship is

that the partner is being unfaithful and carrying on a constant "affair" with someone else. The attempts by the partner to reassure such a person are completely ineffective, and often add to the emotional tension. All kinds of reasonable actions are adduced as "proof," and bitter aggressive recriminations may be made, even for hours on end during the night, the person not allowing the "victim" any opportunity to sleep, even following him into another room to carry on the accusation.

As time goes on the character of the delusions may become more obviously false, for example the idea that neighbors are injuring the person with electric waves, or "thought waves," or the conviction that a group of "super scientists" can "see" everything the person sees and can speak and act through him, or that the person is God's anointed agent to rule the world. There is no limit to the range of these delusions, but their main characteristic is their fixity and lack of change except very slowly over the years.

No successful treatment for the relief of these delusions is at present known, and unless they are of a kind or intensity that would bring a risk of danger to the person or to others it is not often necessary to put the sufferer in hospital. The marital partner therefore finds that it is either necessary to develop some way of accepting and tolerating the fantastic ideas, or else, if the situation becomes impossible to the partner or the children, to break up the marriage. In most cases the partner finds ways of coping with the situation with help for most of the time, and when there are bouts of greater intensity the person may be given some hospital care to tide him over the difficult period. Deluded people are often easier in their minds in the "protected" environment of a mental hospital than they are at home.

In many cases the partner will be able to get some help from the doctor about ways of handling the situation, but sometimes the marriage counselor may be asked about it. In general it is best to accept the feelings and ideas of the deluded person without argument, and say, in effect, "if that is so what do you want to do about it?" This does not mean agreeing with the delusions, or disagreeing with them. When bitter accusations are made it may be best again to say "You think I'm doing so and so?" with no attempt to defend, explain, or argue. It may be necessary to say "We will just have to agree to differ on that." It is not at all necessary to defend oneself against all accusations, or even most accusations. It is better to allow one's life to be its own justification and to allow others to think unjustly if they have made up their minds.

With steady and patient and non-retaliatory handling, and with acceptance of the deluded person, it is often possible to carry on, and sometimes the delusions seem to become less intense over the years, although with periods of greater pressure at times. But it always demands great restraint and devotion, and a firmness that carries on one's own life calmly in spite of the attempts to upset it. Marriage counselors can sometimes help the partner greatly in this.

It seems clear then that when any form of physical or mental illness becomes a threat to the preservation of a good marital relationship the counselor's task is in two directions. It is first to recognize that an illness exists by having some idea of the main indications of illness, and of the various kinds of illness, so that he may recommend appropriate medical help. His second task is to help the sufferer if possible, and even more the partner, to live with the situation if he is willing to do so.

It is certainly not necessary for the counselor who is not a medical practitioner to recognize the exact nature of any illness, nor can he set out to treat any illness. Diagnosis and treatment lie within the field of medicine and it is important for marriage counselors to have close contact with medical consultants of the appropriate kinds, family doctors, physicians, psychiatrists, gynecologists and pediatricians. Conversely marriage counselors can be of great help to doctors because many of the disturbed people who go to doctors for help are found to be suffering from strains and conflicts in marriage which have a material effect on their illness and on the efficacy of any medical treatment. Many people who come to marriage counselors are actually referred to them by doctors.

In the matter of referral to psychiatrists it is wise for a marriage counselor who believes a client needs psychiatric help to refer him first to the client's own family doctor if he has one, and to suggest a list of family doctors from which he can choose if he has no regular doctor. It is then quite appropriate for the family doctor to make a suitable referral. This practice has two important advantages. It is less upsetting to the client to be told that the counselor believes him to be in need of "medical" help than "psychiatric" help. A suggestion that he needs psychiatric help will not always be well accepted from a "layman," and may be regarded as an "accusation" that he is "mental." He will take such referral much better from a medical man. Second, it is often valuable for the psychiatrist to have a family doctor cooperating with him, and possibly available to tide over an emergency when the psychiatrist may not be available. This is best secured by the referral being carried out by the family doctor.

d. *Irreligion* as an intra-personal factor may be distinguished from difference of religious denomination and other forms of religious incompatibility, which are more fittingly considered with the inter-personal factors. Irreligion is difficult to define in simple terms, and it may not necessarily correspond to outward or conventional indications. It may be thought of as a lack of an adequate sense of purpose, and consequently of values; gross self-centeredness and selfishness. In this sense it will obviously make for great strain and difficulty in marriage, which requires some genuine concern for the welfare of others, some willingness to accept and forgive in realistic awareness of one's own fallibility. Professor John MacMurray once observed that "the field of religion is that of human relationships," and the Founder of Christianity laid down one predominant criterion by which the quality of our religion can be tested, "By this shall all men know that ye are my disciples, that ye love one another" (St. John 13:35).

It is not the province of the marriage counselor as such to preach religion to those who come for help. But he may be able to contribute much to such a situation, first through the quality of his own empathy and acceptance of both partners; second, by respecting their own religious attitudes even when they are markedly different from his, and looking with them at the implications of their attitudes with regard to the marriage relationships; and third, through referral to someone who may be able to give constructive help in any religious difficulties which may be recognized. No marriage counselor has any right to use his position to seek to impose any of his own beliefs or attitudes on anyone else. He may "let his light shine" out of himself, but that is quite a different matter from trying to make it shine into any other person.

We have considered four sets of intra-personal factors which can contribute to marital disorder, ignorance (or misinformation), immaturity, illness and irreligion. Although they are primarily intra-personal they cannot help bringing a degree of strain on the relationship. But they generally need to be dealt with mostly on the individual level, sometimes with the help of an appropriate person. As we have seen they are often best helped by a wise referral unless the marriage counselor has some special competence in the field of individual therapy concerned. At the same time the marriage counselor may well have an important role in helping the other partner to live with the disturbed situation while any individual help is being obtained, and possibly when the intra-personal disorder persists in spite of any attempts to help. He may also be able to help two disturbed people to live more peacefully together and to work out some flexible "live and let live" arrangement.

2. SOME INTER-PERSONAL FACTORS WHICH CAN CONTRIBUTE TO MARITAL DISORDER

These are factors which primarily concern the relationship between the partners rather than the specific fitness of either of them for marriage. Those who come into close contact with marital disorders find many examples of people who are individually well developed in every way, and able to get on well with all kinds of people, but yet find themselves in deep and destructive conflict with each other. This has become more common in these days, partly because we expect much more from marriage in happiness and fulfilment than our grandparents seemingly did, and partly because of what is termed "the emancipation of women," because of which they are no longer compelled to put up with tyranny and cruelty through dependence on their husbands. Modern marriage demands much more from the partners than ever before, and there are consequently many more risks of breakdown. Disturbances in the quality of the marital relationship need therefore be considered in relation to the "role perceptions," the "role expectations," and the consequent "role frustrations" of the partners and of modern society. This social and cultural aspect will be dealt with in the next section, on environmental factors in marital disorder.

a. *Incompatibility* is commonly suggested by the partners and by their relatives as "the cause" of marital disorder, and this is made more plausible by the fact that when people find themselves in conflict their differences become intensified and much more distressing. Some attention will first be given to various kinds of incompatibility that are found in marital disorders, and then to the whole question of incompatibility in general.

Sexual incompatibility seems to be very common in marriage, and many couples accept it, though not at all happily, without allowing it to bring their marriage into any great danger. In some marriages it appears to be the primary cause of deepening marital conflict—when, for example, the partners from the beginning find themselves unable to carry out the sexual relationship to any degree of satisfaction and come to feel disillusioned and frustrated, or when their whole attitudes to sex are found to be so different as to seem irreconcilable. In such cases an apparently good personal relationship may become greatly and progressively strained, especially when the two partners have had high expectations about the sexual relationship, and regarded it as the main basis of their partnership.

But in many cases what appears to be sexual incompatibility is really of deeper origin, either in the inter-personal relational area, or even in the intra-personal field already considered.

In the relational area sexual incompatibility may be a manifestation of a deeper personal incompatibility. For example Harry and Helen have reached the point of almost despairing of their marriage, because Helen has been unable to meet anything like all of Harry's persistent demands, even though she has tried all she knows to satisfy him. The situation has now become much worse because she has found evidence of an affair between Harry and one of the girls at the office. They have decided, with the help of some well-meaning friends, that this must be a matter of sexual incompatibility, and that there is little hope of making their marriage work. But they came for counseling, and the counselor was able to look with them behind the apparent point of conflict.

As the picture unfolded it appeared that Harry was the only child of a very insecure marriage. His father had an eye for many attractive women, and took little responsibility in their home. His mother reacted to her husband's neglect by over-coddling and overindulging her son, so that Harry grew up as a "spoiled child" who got everything he wanted. He then fell on his feet in a good job, and was clever—and unscrupulous—enough to get practically everything he wanted there too. Then he met Helen and carried her off her feet, and he got the only girl he ever wanted without any trouble. It was almost inevitable that he should go on to assume that he should get all he wanted in the sexual relationship whenever he wanted it, and that he should resent any "frustration" from his wife when his mother had always given in to him.

Helen, on the other hand, had had a rather sheltered up-bringing, by good but reserved parents, with whom she had never felt free to discuss any of the "facts of life." She had no brothers and no other close "boy friends," and when Harry came along she plunged eagerly into marriage with little or no intellectual or emotional preparation for it. Her difficulties only drove her more deeply into her shell, which made Harry more insistent and aggressive than ever, until finally, like his father before him, he found some "comfort" outside his marriage.

Here is gross incompatibility, but it is not primarily sexual. It is a deep personal incompatibility (Harry being domineering and Helen lacking in confidence), which is using the sexual relationship as a battleground. This is no hair-splitting distinction, because the healing of such a situation has nothing to do with hormones and everything to do with psychology: with the basic assumptions about life and about people that were behind the attitudes of Harry and Helen to each other. These things are much more amenable to change than hormones. Until Harry can "come to earth" about his demands through seeing himself more clearly it will be very difficult for Helen to cope with the situation, for after all love is not fittingly given at pistol point. When Helen too gains better insight into her own attitudes the way will be open for growth to more mature responsiveness. As they each come to better understanding of the other personality they will find themselves more ready to accept and adjust to their differences, but this will need time and patience, and persistence through many apparent setbacks.

In the intra-personal field an apparent sexual incompatibility may be due to the fact that one of the partners has a sexual abnormality with which no normal marriage partner could be compatible. The frankly homosexual man or woman could only be sexually "compatible" with another of the same sex, and there are many impotent men and frigid women whose difficulties lie deep in their own personalities and need to be dealt with there. Some apparently impotent men and frigid women are basically adequate, but are reacting to a disordered personal relationship with their partners, for example, the nervous man who feels that his masculinity is at stake, and is quite potent with a prostitute but quite impotent with his wife, because of her expressed expectations of him.

A further example of sexual incompatibility is found when one of the partners is the victim of grossly abnormal sexual urges or various forms of sexual deviation. These conditions are generally outside the competence of the marriage counselor, and such people are most appropriately referred for any suitable help they are willing to accept.

Personal incompatibility may of course take many different forms, from the superficial "nothing much in common" to the

deepest levels of personality differences. On the more superficial levels it is often found that the partners gradually drift
further apart because they each become more and more involved in individual interests and fail to preserve or cultivate
any worthwhile interests in common. This is one kind of inattention to the marriage, which will be dealt with later.

Another kind of personal incompatibility may be due to
different levels of intelligence or education, especially when
either partner is emotionally immature to the extent of being
unable to avoid jealousy of the more advanced one. This is
generally more common in our culture when the wife is much
more intellectually advanced than the husband, and even though
she loves him deeply and avoids anything that could be con-
strued as "rubbing it in," he finds it difficult to avoid feelings
of inferiority, however able and successful he may be in his
own field. This is important in pre-marital counseling, mainly
for its recognition and for the awareness of the need for development of emotional maturity and psychic security so that
acceptance is easier. With careful help this kind of difficulty
can often be overcome by the partners.

There may also be gross differences between the partners
regarding the principles and methods of child management,
which may contribute much to marital disorder. The attitudes
of many people to such things are derived more than they may
realize from what they absorbed in their own upbringing, and
to that extent they are not quite fully open to "sweet reason."
Ideally such questions should be faced before marriage, and at
least before the arrival of the first child, so that they can
present a "united front" to the children. But this is often not
done, and arguments, backed by "righteous indignation" grow
more and more intense. The fact that children may suffer far
more from the constant parental conflicts than from the kind
of management either parent would employ does not seem to

penetrate the emotionally disturbed minds of the parents until the emotional tensions are "unbottled" fully in good counseling. In some cases the conflict regarding child management is not what it seems, but rather a deep emotional conflict between the partners which fixes itself on any available battleground. As they unburden their feelings fully this will often become clear, and until it does, to the partners as well as the counselor, the fights will go on.

Another form of personal incompatibility may be found in the various kinds of "mixed marriage," between Christian and non-Christian, between Roman Catholic and Anglican, Episcopal, or Protestant, and even at times between two closely related Protestant denominations. People's denominational and religious attitudes are largely accidents of birth, and they are imbedded so deeply as to be often out of the range of reason. Here again the trouble is not so much the difference, although this has difficulties in it especially with training of children. The trouble is mainly on the level of emotional immaturity, which brings intolerance and attempts at domination or the imposition of religious attitude on the partner. Such differences need competent counseling if they are to be faced in the light of reality and resolved to the extent of mutual acceptance. The same principles apply, sometimes to an even greater extent, in the case of marked racial and cultural differences, especially when there are also color differences.

Deeper (though not necessarily more intense) than any of these "acquired" differences which may make for personal incompatibility are inborn "temperamental" differences of personality type, which may have much to do with marital disorder, especially when, as often, they are not understood and accepted.

Here, for example, are Tom and Betty, married for four years, with two children. They have apparently been in increasing conflict almost from the beginning of their marriage. Now that they look back on it, the conflicts were there during their engagement, but they thought that it would be easy to work them out after their marriage.

There are masses of complaints on both sides, but they seem to be reducible to fairly definite differences. Tom's main complaint about Betty is that she is so utterly careless and irresponsible that he is continually worried that he will be reduced to bankruptcy in his finances and humiliation with his friends. Betty on the other hand takes the view that there's no such problem at all except in Tom's imagination, and that he makes so much of a fuss about every decision that she is driven to desperation. When she wants to invite her friends to their home Tom does his best to dissuade her; or if they do come he behaves in a most ungracious manner, or retires into his den, which she feels is insulting.

As the stories unfold it soon becomes clear that Betty is what Jung called an extrovert type of personality, completely natural and spontaneous, friendly to everyone, and impulsive in almost everything she does. Tom has to admit that even with her impulsiveness she has so far proved that her judgment or "intuition" is sound, and that his deep apprehensiveness is not based on any previous failure on her part. But he finds her intolerant of his need to take time to think out all the different aspects of any proposition or decision, and also of his rooted suspicion of the motives of people whom she "just knows" are good and reliable.

Tom is an accountant, who is building up a first class professional reputation for his reliability and conscientiousness, and he has his office imbued with these great principles. He is not a good mixer, but he has the respect of his associates and clients, and feels content and competent in his work. In other words he is an introvert type of personality in Jung's classification. He had always been shy of girls as he grew up, but Betty's spontaneous friendliness and charm overcame his shyness to the point that he proposed to her, and she was attracted by his conscientious and steady nature; he was so different from many of the boys who had tried to sweep her off her feet. They got on very well together until they found themselves in the intimate relationship of marriage, and then each began to find the attitudes of the other difficult to accept.

It is possible that with some encouragement Tom might develop more sociability, and Betty might tone down some of her impulsiveness, but these qualities of extroversion and introversion are deeply imbedded in Betty's and Tom's personalities and are not open to radical change. But with better understanding each can learn to accept the other, and to be more responsive to the better aspects of each other's personalities.

Other types of personality which may bear on marriage are the "schizoid" or suspicious type, the obsessional or very particular, the "mercurial" or "cyclothyme," and the "hysteric" or over-dramatic. Tom had some obsessional and schizoid elements in his personality. The way to better marital harmony is through acceptance of each other's personality types.

It seems obvious that in any consideration of incompatibility we must face the fact that it is a matter of degree, depending on what amount and intensity of difference people can tolerate. The word "compatible" comes from two Latin words and means "able to suffer with," or "endure together." There are obviously limits as to what can be endured together in marriage, but there are some considerations about incompatibility that are most relevant to marriage counseling.

The first is that people do not necessarily have to remain as they are. Sick marriages, like sick persons, can often be healed if given some help. It seems clear that any help is more likely to succeed when the underlying factors in the incompatibility are discovered and dealt with, and the plausible rationalizations are honestly faced. Many examples of "incompatibility" are more fittingly regarded as intolerance and these can only be dealt with when this is faced and accepted. Others as we have seen are not of the same kind as they appear, and "sexual incompatibility" may be a manifestation of personal incompatibility, in which case it needs to be dealt with from the personal rather than the sexual point of view.

Secondly the whole question needs to be seen in relation to the fact that if any two partners were completely "compatible" their marriage would become intolerably dull. Within the limits of what can be endured together, incompatibility provides a source of mutual interest, and a challenge to continued mutual exploration rather than an excuse for writing it off as hopeless. The good counselor may help the partners to learn to accept each other's different feelings and attitudes, even the hostile ones; and each other's conduct within the law. At the same time one of them may learn to keep on contributing what he can to the relationship, even when the other one seems to be doing very little about it.

b. *Intolerance, indifference and inattention* to the marriage relationship are put together because they are different expressions of lack of the "goodwill" or the "we" feeling which is essential for happy marriage.

Intolerance, already mentioned, means a refusal to allow one's partner the normal autonomy or "self-government" which we have come to regard as an essential part of our democratic way of life. Of course there must be limits to tolerance, and refusal to allow such illegal actions as cruelty, theft, or adultery is not only justifiable, but an essential aspect of good partnership. But it is very common to find in marital disorders that one or both partners are trying to mold the other into an arbitrary kind of personality pattern, and being demanding and dictatorial about matters that are not essentially of common concern.

These possessive dictatorial attitudes are often found to be signs of deep psychic insecurity and fear of being dominated, frustrated or humiliated, and in such cases they are neurotic attitudes which may need help. Sometimes intolerance is simply the "carry over" into marriage of a "spoiled child" attitude.

Intolerance may show itself in many different ways. There may be outbursts of temper, and aggressive demands with moodiness and sulking when they are not fulfilled. There may be "righteous indignation" with the conviction that it is possible to hold another person up to his "moral obligations." There may be persistent nagging, "the chief weapon of the weak against the strong," or jealousy and bitterness. And there may even be suffering or illness for the purpose (generally unconscious) of "blackmailing" the partner to conform to the person's wishes or demands.

Indifference may be described as lack of interest in the partner's welfare in all its aspects, attitudes, interests, doings, and in the partnership itself. This may arise from the feeling of being threatened in status or control, from preoccupation with selfish affairs, or from deeply imbedded individualism and self-centeredness. It may also be a result of despair about the marriage. The really self-centered are generally poor candidates for marriage unless they can see themselves to a sufficient extent to develop beyond their self-worship. But they often get married in the blind assumption that all their needs will be met by a devoted partner, who is generally unaware of these great expectations and soon comes to rebel when they become obvious. Indifference is the true opposite of goodwill, just as hatred is the opposite of the emotional aspect of love. When marriage and the family are not given a high priority in the attitudes of both partners it is inevitable that their standards will drift into dull monotonous mediocrity or incessant wearing conflict.

Inattention to the marriage relationship is often an expression of indifference, but it is just as often due to ignorance or immaturity. Young people do not always realize that love is a living quality, and that it therefore needs constant nourishment. It can only be nourished by being expressed and received, by word and gesture, by thoughtful kindly spontaneous actions, and deepest of all through the mutual self-offering of a devoted sexual relationship. Marriage needs constant daily work from both partners if it is to be kept alive and fresh, and when the marriage and one's partner are "taken for granted" the marriage must suffer to some extent. Neglect from whatever cause throws a big strain on it.

c. *Immorality* includes much more than infidelity and adultery. It also includes such common enemies of partnership as dishonesty, untruthfulness, cruelty, mental as well as physical, extreme meanness and many other similar kinds of attitude and behavior. One of the essential obligations of people in any kind of partnership, even in business partnership, is that they should "play the game." This is equally true, though much less enforceable, in the marriage partnership, and although adultery is one of the most common grounds for divorce, many of the other kinds of immorality may be strong factors in marital disorder and breakdown. The situation is made more difficult by the fact that almost any kind of immorality is apt to lead to reactions on the part of the offended partner that may also extend to immorality. While there seems no reason why any wife or husband should have to put up with unlimited injury and insult, the fallibility of all human beings would seem to warrant a reasonable tolerance of both sides and a willingness to forgive in the realization of the fact that none of us is so without sin as to be fit to cast stones. Failure to forgive in this same sense may do as much harm to a marriage partnership as many other kinds of immorality.

Perhaps it is worth reminding ourselves that although marriage is quite dependent on the quality of love that exists between the partners there are times and situations in which it is difficult if not impossible to love, at least in the "feeling" sense of the relationship. But fidelity, being a matter of the will, is possible to anyone with mature disciplined self-control, even though at times it may be difficult. To stand firmly together through the difficult times, even though it may seem to be "flying blind," and at the same time seeking help and giving it time to work, may be the real salvation of a marital disorder.

3. SOME ENVIRONMENTAL FACTORS WHICH CAN CONTRIBUTE TO MARITAL DISORDER

There is very substantial agreement among those who come into close contact with marital disorder that the intra-personal and inter-personal difficulties already considered, and possibly others related to them, are frequent factors in marital disorder. But it is becoming more and more realized that they do not explain nearly all of the marital disorders. Some American sociologists are asking whether these factors can adequately explain the high rate of marriage dissolution in the United States as compared with that in other countries.

For example—does the neighboring country of Canada, with only one fifth the divorce rate of the U.S.A., have such a high standard of personal fitness and so high a quality of personal relationships that only one fifth of their people, proportionately, are unfit for marriage? Does Britain, another industrialized country, have only one quarter proportionately of people unfit for marriage as compared with the United States, where the divorce rate is four times as great?

One must of course allow for differences in divorce legislation in any such comparisons, but the difference would seem to be more significant than the actual differences in legislation would account for. (And, of course, this very difference may be regarded as an environmental factor to be reckoned with in marital disorder.)

But we have also to consider the great increase in the divorce rate over the last half century in many countries, and to ask ourselves whether this could be explained by any comparable decrease in personal fitness for marriage or any comparable corruption in people's capacity for close personal relationships.

These interesting considerations have led to an increasing amount of concentration on the environmental factors, particularly the sociological, in marital disorder, in the realization also that marriage is a living relationship in two-way interaction with the environment, and therefore inevitably affected by it. The home and family in fact can be attacked by influences from outside in the same way as people can be attacked by germs and other noxious agents from outside.

The environmental factors may be considered from the point of view of the different aspects of the marital environment, physical, personal, social and cultural, and spiritual.

a. *Physical environment.* Here we may think of such various influences as housing, neighborhood resources, financial arrangements, and equipment.

Cramped, uncomfortable and otherwise unsuitable housing, lacking in opportunities for desired privacy or in playing space for children, may well add greatly to the burdens of marriage, especially when there is ill health, fatigue or other reason for extra strain. Situations of this kind often have to be endured by young, newly married, often immature partners, who have had no opportunity to settle down properly together and forge a strong enough union to be able to bear these burdens; and it is all too easy for them to be brought to the point of despair as a result. This was particularly true during the post-World War II years.

Deficiencies in such neighborhood resources as shops, kindergartens, schools, churches, community centers, parks and other recreational facilities, lack of adequate transportation resources, and lack of such amenities as home help and baby sitters, may also add heavy burdens to a young couple compelled to live in such unsuitable areas because of the requirements of jobs or because of financial stringencies. Here again the situation is more difficult for people who have not had the opportunity to establish real partnership or to put down adequate roots in their community. Some rapidly developing "new housing areas" are taking these factors into more consideration in these days, but in other cases they are showing little evidence of so doing. The cramped apartment living in many large cities, with few available recreational amenities, would appear to provide many extra strains for marriage and family life. When children have only the streets to play on, and when the streets are ruled by some form of gangsterism, the community is breeding more and more delinquency for the future, as well as making marital disorder more frequent.

There are some financial factors which make for difficulty in marriage. Financial stringency can be a very heavy burden unless there are some reasonable expectations of relief. In some cases the financial stringency is the result of foolish spending on unnecessary things, or on gambling or drinking or even drugs in some cases, but then the marital disorder is more appropriately tackled from the point of view of the personality disorder behind the overspending. In other cases there are deep conflicts about the financial arrangements of the partnership, and often these are the expression of a deep emotional conflict which fastens itself on anything that can be used as a battleground. In these cases no great relief from the marital disorder is likely until this underlying emotional conflict, or this battle for emotional domination, is honestly faced.

It is an interesting and tragic comment on human nature that many marital disorders seems to be traceable to the fact of too much money as a factor in the trouble. Here of course it is not really the excess of money that causes the trouble but the immaturity, selfishness or similar personal disorder that makes it difficult to cope with excess wealth. The good counselor will try to help the partners to the achievement of some insight about these deeper elements of the problem.

Domestic furnishings and equipment have some part to play in the general comfort and "homeliness" of the living arrangements, and this is necessarily related with the financial resources of the couple, with the steadiness and permanence of the husband's and wife's jobs (which allow more indulgence in "time payment"), and also with questions of priority and agreement in what the available resources are to be spent on. Here again the real problem is often an underlying personal or relational one.

When these factors concerning the physical environment come up in counseling it is therefore the counselor's task to gain some idea of any underlying personal and relational factors that might have brought the housing, financial and other difficulties about, or might be making them persistent or destructive to the marriage. At the same time it may be possible to refer them to some available and suitable social agency which may be able to help in the crisis and to assist them to better ways of promoting their marital and family welfare.

b. *The personal environment of marriage.* This is a possible source of many marital difficulties. "Interfering in-laws," especially when any of them live with or very near the partners, have been a well known source of trouble. The seductive charm of "the girl at the office" or "the man at the office" is also well known. Many a so-called "friend" has exerted a disruptive influence on a marriage partnership, and so have neighbors, job associates, "gangs," and other personal interferences.

But it seems clear that just as the resistance of the human body is an important factor in germ infection, so the "resistance" of the marriage relationship is an important factor in the marital "infection." When some personal interference is found to be an apparent causative factor in a marital disorder the counselor will generally have no contact with, and certainly no influence, on the source of the interference, so he can then only help by trying to strengthen the "resistance" of the marriage to such attempts at interference.

For example, when a mother-in-law seems to be dominating one of the partners, the counselor can generally do nothing with her—even if it were regarded as the right way to deal with the situation, which is seldom if ever the case. The dominated partner, however, will need some help designed to bring insight into the reasons for allowing such domination, and the constructive ways of recovering the kind of mature autonomy which is necessary for a good adult partnership.

In many other cases of interference there is an underlying defect in the marriage which makes it, or one of the partners, vulnerable to such outside attractions or pressures. There may have been long and wearing conflict, lack of attention to the marriage with indifference and neglect, persistent loneliness and monotony, or any other similar disease of the marriage. Sometimes such chronic disease, like disease in the human body, is "walled off" from everyday interaction, but yet it may gradually corrode the marriage and make it susceptible to any external destructive influence.

Another aspect of the personal environmental influences is the type of job being carried out by one or both partners. When there is inescapable job dissatisfaction it will inevitably have its influence on the marital relationship, as of course disturbed domestic relationships will have their influence on the quality and satisfaction of a person's daily work. It may be too that an inescapable job involves long or difficult hours, undue worry or strain, or prolonged absence from home. It may also make it impossible for a family to settle down for any length of time in one place because it entails constant moving from place to place. These difficulties add to the strains of domestic life, and may often be revealed during counseling. When the external difficulties cannot be altered it is then the task of the counselor to help the partners to work out possible ways of working better together within the limits laid down by these vocational necessities.

c. *The social and cultural environment of marriage.* Under this general heading we can profitably consider a large number of different external environmental factors which may contribute in a direct or in a very subtle way to marital discord and even disaster.

In general it may be said that the rapid change over the last half century in society, in culture, and not least in technology, has possibly had as great an influence on marriage as on any other social institution. Most of the factors about to be described are linked closely with this rapid change. As already mentioned, marriage and family life cannot be unrelated to social realities, and rapid change will always bring periods of strain and conflict between old and new, and challenges to adaptation to the new situation. In such a close personal relationship as marriage, with its deep emotional involvements, there are bound to be distressing tensions in the process.

One of the most radical and far-reaching of these changes has been the emancipation of women. Fifty years ago few women were trained to any kind of occupation that would make them financially independent, and it was rare for a woman to enjoy the social independence of a "bachelor's flat" in the middle of a big city. As a result wives were generally so dependent on their husbands that even if they suffered greatly in marriage they were compelled to make the best of it. Today almost all women are trained in some occupation through which they can be financially independent, and large numbers of single women, together with widows and divorced or "separated" women, live alone and carry on a full life with complete social acceptance. As a result of this great change there is no essential reason, except for the needs of children, why any woman should put up with continued cruelty or persecution in marriage. This emancipation is the social fulfillment of an ideal to which people have paid lip service for many centuries; the essential dignity of human personality, male and female, and it provides one of the greatest challenges to marriage.

The immediate result of the emancipation of women is that marriage has been raised to a higher status, an equal partnership carried on by mutual consent by two free autonomous people. At the same time it is inevitably more difficult, and demands more from the partners, than ever before. The great increase in the breakdown rate over the last half century is more probably due to the increased standard of marriage than to any great decrease in the competence and character of people.

This social change is something that no marriage counselor can or would wish to alter, but it has a vital effect on the whole work of helping to promote better marriage. Most importantly of all, it has brought a vital new need into the forefront of human affairs: the need for first-class, comprehensive and universal preparation for marriage, from earliest childhood onwards. And marriage counselors are in the forefront of this great future social project, designed to help all people to become as fit as possible for the conduct of modern marriage, and so prevent so many of its disorders from happening. The other great effect on the work of marriage counselors is that it includes the consideration with each of the conflicting partners of the main essential conditions of such an equal partnership between free autonomous people. Many of them have inherited from their own upbringing an out-of-date concept of marriage as a male-dominated "autocracy" or dictatorship, and this uncritical assumption may be very difficult for some husbands to grow out of.

Another social factor in marital disorder is found in the prevailing social ideas, values, customs and practices in the community. Such matters as the current practices regarding "dating" and courtship, and the earlier age at which people tend to marry, may have much to do with later difficulties—especially when combined with the current tendency to individualism, which makes partnership more difficult and vulnerable when the partners feel frustrated in their desire to get more than they give. It is often difficult for people conditioned by the highly competitive acquisitive atmosphere of the business and even the professional world to reorient themselves to the mutual consideration and self-offering so necessary in marriage, unless they have been very strongly conditioned in this unselfish, habitual attitude. This may be one reason why many people who have proved their competence and even brilliance in the business or professional world have proved to be utterly incompetent as marital partners and parents.

At the same time our present way of life has led to much specialization and "compartmentalization," possibly necessary for efficiency in the many complex technicalities of modern life. But this has so far not been balanced by sufficient training in the arts and the humanities for full personal development. The result is a lessening of human communication in social contacts, and therefore a lessening in human understanding. This is often made worse by social conventions which separate the sexes, through which men and women form separate groups at social gatherings, and feel ill at ease in ordinary social discussion, which therefore tends to be superficial and trivial.

In some countries also young people are forced to a separation between the sexes during the important school years, from the ages of five or six to as old as eighteen or twenty, which deprives them of some practice in the art of social relationships to the possible detriment of their later spontaneity and self-control in friendship, courtship, mate-selection and marriage. Here again these factors are mainly relevant to the fuller preparation for marriage which is so necessary in our present situation.

At the same time as the lessening of emotional and intellectual communication between men and women there is a much greater "throwing together" of men and women in their daily work. As a result of this many a man or woman may have as many or more interests in common with colleagues and associates at work than with the partner at home. This of course need not happen if the partners set out to cultivate and practice common interests, but if they fail to forge bonds of this kind the shared interests with someone of the opposite sex outside the home may tend to compete with the marital relationship and eventually destroy it.

Another important change in the social and cultural environment is the development to universal availability of scientific contraception. This has completed the emancipation of women, and saved them from many unwanted pregnancies. Families have tended to become smaller, more "selective," and when young people have larger families it is generally because they want them. This makes for more contentment in the marriage partnership and has in many ways strengthened it.

(It has also made it possible for people to indulge in sexual intercourse outside marriage with much less fear of pregnancy, and this is always a potential or actual threat to the stability of marriage. At the same time the progress of medical science has greatly diminished the fear of venereal disease, and this has also increased the temptation to illicit sexual relationships.)

Parallel with these social and cultural changes of the twentieth century is the progressive concentration of more and more people in large cities, with all the drawbacks as well as the advantages of urbanization. People of greatly different cultural and racial backgrounds are thrown into close social and cultural contact, and this is intensified by the vast growth of transport facilities.

This development has had many effects on marriage and family life. In the past young people mostly met and married partners from their own neighborhoods, and of reasonably similar cultural and racial background. Their respective parents also generally knew each other well, and the marriages began with fairly sound roots. In these days, however, young people often meet and marry partners from much more varied backgrounds and from much greater distances because of availability of public and private transport and of telephone communication. Their respective parents may not have even seen each other until the wedding day, and sometimes not even then, and the young people may well begin their marriage with practically no social roots. Their differences of culture, class, religion, or even race may seem of little account when they are "in love," but they all too often prove to be a very great handicap to the development of unity when the "glamor" has worn off in the grim realities of everyday living together.

Apart from such differences of family background there is also much greater likelihood in these days of unsound family backgrounds in one or both partners. This has been found by many investigators to be one of the very common factors in marital disorder and breakdown. At the 1959 Annual Conference of the British Medical Association Dr. H. V. Dicks of London reported that he and his collaborators had studied 157 disturbed marriages, and compared their findings with a control group of happy marriages. In the maritally disturbed group the marriage partners were predominantly of high social status and education: four fifths owned their own houses or flats. Of 299 spouses, no fewer than 239 came from broken homes or homes with poor parental relations, where there was violence between the parents, temporary desertion, and so on. Only 4.2% of the spouses came from emotionally good homes.

In contrast, in the matched control group, 54.6% came from good homes. The 299 spouses showed few overt neurotic symptoms, but disturbed parental relations in the home when the spouses weer children seemed very significant, and under certain conditions the spouses seemed to enact a compulsive repetition of their childhood experience. One of the conditions seemed to be their age. It seemed that marriages came to a crisis when the partners reached 35 or so, when the children were off to school. Dr. Dicks thought this mid-term crisis might be partly physiological (hormonal ageing), or partly the consequence of middle-class people having become isolated within the family group and demanding more of marriage and the family than they could give. (British Medical Journal, Sept. 26, 1959, page 567.)

In addition to its value in elucidating factors in marital disorder, this and similar investigations provide much support for the view that any project which helps in the betterment of present day marriages will have many positive effects on marriages in the future, by equipping more young people with the emotional and personal resources for the achievement of a satisfactory marriage.

In some countries the marital situation has been made still more difficult because of much greater mobility of families than in earlier times, with greater difficulty in laying down roots to increase their solidarity in the face of the stresses and strains of modern urban life. New social organizations seem to be needed, and in many places are being created, to provide better opportunities for family consolidation.

Much of this mobility arises from the necessity of earning a living in a country in which many jobs involve frequent change of domicile. In addition to these movements of necessity there are probably many which arise more from insatiable ambition than from necessity, in which social status is felt to depend on advancement and "success," and which must therefore be pursued, whatever the cost. In such cases the disturbing factor is more personal than environmental.

Another fact of our time which has profound influence on marriage, as on almost every aspect of modern life, is the mass media—radio and television, the press, the cinema, the paper-back book, the magazine and the novel, the theatre, and modern mass advertising in all its intrusive channels. These, with their blatant and subtly suggestive emphasis on seductive charm and superficial "popularity," based on possessions and external appearance and posturing rather than on genuine warmth and goodwill, add greatly to the problems of young married people as they "come down to earth," often with painful disillusionment.

The extent of the influence of mass-media communications in our culture is quite beyond assessment. There is no doubt that they provide a very subtle and painless form of brain washing, repeated day after day from the time when a child is first able to comprehend to the time of senility or death.

The fact that other victims of the brain washing reiterate the superficial ideas gives a kind of "feed-back" quality to the original ubiquitous influence, increasing its effect to a still more alarming extent.

The total effect on marriage of the persistent emphasis on sensuality, or gratification of appetite and other forms of self-centeredness, and on the superficial emotional aspects of human relationships, is yet unmeasured. But one apparent aspect of this is the molding of people into a cultural pattern in which competitiveness and conformity seem to go hand in hand, in which a significant part of our western culture has been drawn from the "tradition directed" and the much more civilized "inner directed" influence to the "other directed" attitudes which would convert human communities to something comparable with flocks of sheep. The terms have been borrowed from David Riesman's book "The Lonely Crowd" (Doubleday, 1953).

Another effect of this enormous growth of the mass media is the more general acceptance of the idea of divorce, with much less associated sense of failure and guilt. This has profound effects on marriage and family life. One of its consequences is that people tend increasingly to marry, thinking of marriage as some kind of trial partnership, which can easily be scrapped if it fails to "work out." This constitutes a threat to "the sanctity of marriage," in that people then tend to marry with much less sense of responsibility and more from "gratification of appetite." The result must be increasing incidence of marital failure if it is not faced and dealt with by better education and preparation for marriage and parenthood. This is a much more constructive way than trying to prevent divorce in cases where a marriage has obviously broken down beyond hope of repair. On the credit side of acceptance of divorce is the attention given to protection of children from the strains of parental divorce, which may help them in their eventual marriages.

With the increasing acceptance of divorce there is also an increasing social and even political acceptance of "de facto" wives, which tends to add to the disorganization of marriage, however "expedient" it may be in any particular case. It is not the counselor's business to moralize or to interfere in any such relationship, but rather to help to promote better harmony for those who seek his help, whatever may be the kind of marital relationship they may choose to participate in. In some cases however the interests of the rejected wife or husband may be helped by inviting consideration of the ultimate possibilities of what the "de facto" partners are contemplating, but this can only be done in an atmosphere of acceptance and permissiveness, unless the counselor is determined to exceed his prerogatives.

At the national level the creation of what has been called "The Welfare State" may have striking effects on marriage. In Australia, for example, where pensions and social benefits have increased over the years to the point of reasonably workable social security, the institution of pensions for "deserted wives" seems to have brought about a great increase in the number of deserting husbands. It would appear that many of these deserting husbands have been "encouraged" to leave by the knowledge that their wives will be assisted by the Government, and this is already constituting a serious problem for the Government social welfare organizations.

Behind all of these social and cultural changes of our time there is the constant menacing threat of overwhelming world conflict, following on the two great world wars and the uneasy peace that occupied the years between them. The revolutionary discoveries of atomic physics and the increasing conquests of space, together with the astronomical expenditure on these things and on defense, have also had their effects on marriage. Among other effects are those consequent on the enormous expenditure on defense, which involves heavy taxation and the diversion of manpower into fields that are unproductive when considered against housing and other social amenities. The general unrest, a product of incessant underlying anxiety, has probably made for more nervousness and less flexibility in domestic relationships. It may be that the human race will have to live with these difficulties for some time to come, and this is also a challenge to marriage, which at its best can provide the best of all havens of peace for the "recreation" of tired strained personalities.

d. *The spiritual environmental factors in marital disorder.* What might be called "the spiritual climate of marriage" has a very profound (but not easy to describe) influence on marriage, and in trying to give some account of it one must consider not so much the spiritual attitudes of the partners, as the general spiritual attitudes of the community.

It seems reasonable, at the risk of superficiality, to suggest that such spiritual values as love, generosity, and consideration have been to some extent replaced by utilitarian values and matters of expediency. This is not to underestimate the generosity of millions of people in the face of calamity and need, and the unassuming "good neighborliness" of people everywhere. But many of the disorders of marriage stem from the fact that partners allow selfish interests to take priority over the mutual interests of the partnership, the family, and the wider interests of the community. One reason for this in many cases is that they have grown up in a spiritual climate in which the values that are most essential to sound marriage and family life are largely ignored or even discredited. When children are brought up wisely, fully aware of the love of two parents who love each other and accept each other—even when the parents do not "understand" each other—the children yet receive the most essential spiritual nourishment for the growth of their own personalities. Such outgoing unselfish love, which radiates outward also from the family into the community, can only be sustained and deepened when it is continually nourished through some adequate kind of worship, whether this be according to conventional patterns or not.

In many ways the Church has lost some of its leadership in the community to secular organizations, and it has all too often failed to rise to the newest needs of the community. For example, its general emphasis on the indissolubility of marriage would seem to imply a sacred obligation to take a much more vigorous lead in the community towards better preparation for marriage. At the same time such leadership in the promotion of better home and family living would constitute the greatest possible contribution that could be made in these days towards the prevention of mental illness, and such "social illness" as delinquency, vandalism and crime. If it be true that the most influential of all known and controllable causes of mental and social illness is the deprivation of the right kind of love and security in childhood in the home, then the Church has a greater potential contribution to this great social project than any other body, the medical profession included.

This would seem to call for full consideration at the highest level—offering one of the greatest opportunities for united creative leadership that has ever been open to the Church.

There are many signs of growing interest and greater co-operation between the different branches of the Church, in what could be the most effective evangelistic opportunity of all time, the strengthening of the home life of the nation.

When the family is strengthened in these different ways it will soon recover much that has been lost with regard to its vital work of preparing people for future marriage. The homes of the future are in a very real sense being made or marred in the homes of today. With the recovery of family traditions the family itself will provide, as it used to do, some of the most influential and enduring preparation for sound marriage, and the influence will go on into the next and still more of the future generations.

CHAPTER III

The Marriage Counselor

I. WHAT KINDS OF PEOPLE MIGHT BE INVOLVED IN MARRIAGE COUNSELING?

As MARRIAGE is a universal institution, and marital disorders of a severity requiring help are almost as widespread, it is inevitable that almost anybody might become involved in some kind of attempt to assist in the reconciliation of marital conflicts. Many people will be emotionally involved as in-laws and other relatives; others may be less involved, such as good friends and neighbors, but still prone to take sides, to criticize or condemn, to advise, and in many cases to interfere on their own initiative. Even if some of these people have a so-called good practical knowledge of marriage, from their own direct or indirect experience, they still have had no adequate training in marriage counseling, and as we have seen their most sincere and devoted efforts are not likely to be of much permanent benefit. But they may have a valuable part in the reconciliation if they can be content to exert some influence towards the obtaining of more competent help.

Apart from these interested parties, what kinds of people might be or become involved in marriage counseling? If we survey the field in various countries the people who may find themselves in the role of counselor or conciliator in either an informal or a formal way may be divided into several groups for the purpose of discussion.

a. *People with some training and experience in dealing with other people in a personal way, but with little or no specific training in counseling or in the principles of personal or marital relationships.* Under this group heading we can include many ministers, doctors, teachers, lawyers, probation officers, magistrates, sociologists, welfare officers, personnel officers, military, naval and air force officers, youth leaders, and many others in positions of leadership. These people may often be brought into contact with marital disorders in the course of their daily work, especially if they are interested in people and sensitive to signs of anxiety and other kinds of emotional tension. A large amount of quiet, unobtrusive help is being given by such people in many cases of marital trouble, and it is probable that such help is often enough to prevent some early and less serious difficulties from further deterioration. It is hoped that some of the insights expressed in this book may possibly help such relatively untrained helpers to develop more and more adequate ways of serving those who come into their orbit.

b. *People who are professionally trained in interviewing, and possibly in counseling and even psychotherapy, but who have had little specific training in marriage counseling.* This group includes psychiatrists, psychologists, social workers, (especially psychiatric social workers), and ministers and sociologists with special training in counseling. From their training and experience such people are sometimes more likely to see the marital disorders which come their way from the point of view of the intra-personal difficulties of each partner than from that of the inter-personal relationship, which is the primary, though not the exclusive concern of the marriage counselor as such. When they have become oriented to the "inter-personal relationship" point of view, and have equipped themselves with adequate knowledge of the principles and inner dynamics of the marriage relationship, they are then able to be of very great help indeed in marital problems, as consultants as well as counselors.

c. *People who are professionally trained in interviewing and counseling as well as in their own professional activities, and have added to this an adequate special training in the principles and inner dynamics of marriage and family life.* Such people may be well equipped to provide a professional marriage counseling service of high quality.

This is the goal toward which the American Association of Marriage Counselors is moving, and the membership of that association, for which stringent conditions are necessarily imposed, is made up of members of several professions who have undertaken special training and secured considerable experience in the whole marital field. In 1957 it was made up of social workers, 20%; doctors, 19% (gynecologists 8%, general medicine 6%, and psychiatrists 5%); educators, 16%; ministers, 15%; psychologists, 14%; sociologists, 12%; and lawyers, 4%. ("Marriage Counseling: A Case Book" Association Press, New York, 1958, page 485.)

These professional people, and others who are similarly trained but are not members of the Association, carry out their work either as members of a marriage counseling or social welfare agency, an educational or psychiatric foundation or clinic, or a religious organization; or individually as private practitioners. There are some first class training centers in the United States, whose graduates are gradually spreading across the country. There are also opportunities for some professional training in Great Britain and in other countries.

d. *People without any particular professional background or training, who have been very carefully selected from the point of view of their personal integrity and intelligence, their emotional maturity and balance, and their ability to undertake and make use of special training.* Such people have been recruited to an increasing extent in Great Britain and more recently in Australia and New Zealand from the point of view of ability to give their voluntary part time services to marriage counseling when trained and "accredited," through marriage counseling agencies and under supervision. For various reasons the selection is limited to those who are or have been happily married and not divorced or separated, and very careful assessment is continuously carried on throughout their training regarding their fitness for the work. At the end of their training course, which is full and comprehensive, they are assessed again and if satisfactory are "accredited" as "provisional counselors" or "associate counselors." They are then given a further period of "in-service training," after which, if satisfactory to the assessors, they are accredited as marriage counselors on the staff of the particular marriage counseling agency or one related with it.

This "lay" approach to marriage counseling, which is not found to any extent in America, has gradually emerged in response to increasingly urgent needs and a much greater shortage of professionally trained people than existed in America. Even if all the available professionally trained people could have been diverted to marriage counseling, which of course was impossible, this would still have failed to meet the needs of the situation or to come within the financial resources of the countries. "A new resource," as Professor David Mace described it in England, had to be mobilized, trained, and put to work. With their genius for voluntary social services the people of Great Britain were pioneers in this great social project, and from 1942 onward it has developed and extended in a manner that has more than fulfilled the most optimistic hopes of its imitators and overcome the doubts of the skeptics. It has also received unqualified commendation from the British

Royal Commission on Marriage and Divorce, 1951-3 (London, H.M.S.O., 1956).

It is essential, however, to emphasize the conditions which are found to be necessary for such a service to be successfully carried out. Careful and continuous "selection" and screening, full and comprehensive training, followed by "in-service" training, expert and comprehensive assessment of suitability, the fullest safeguards of team work under the competent supervision of professionally trained and experienced "case supervisors," and the full backing of a carefully selected panel of professional "consultants" to whom clients in need of any special help can be referred and with whom the counselors can consult in any case of difficulty.

It seems certain that this approach to marriage counseling as a voluntary part-time social service will continue and expand in countries in which it has been operating. The lack of sufficient available professional resources, and the cost of such resources even if they were available, would seem to make this inevitable. But more important still is the fact that this approach has abundantly proved its success wherever it has been carried out under the already mentioned safeguards. It seems clear that the greater the extension of this work the more efficient and available the professional supervision and the consultant's panels will need to be.

e. *Consultants*. These are professionally trained people of special competence in an appropriate field related to marriage, who are willing to see clients referred to them, generally at their own professional rooms or offices, as a private professional service under a mutually acceptable financial arrangement. Included among them are those who are especially competent in the counseling and psychotherapeutic fields, such as psychiatrists, psychologists, and some pastors and social workers. There will be others who may have little or no training or experience in the psychological areas, but are expert in some limited field, such as gynecology, urology, medicine, pediatrics, social casework, law, ethics, religion, vocational guidance or child guidance.

It seems desirable, and it often happens, that these people should have some continuous contact with the marriage counseling agency with which they work, and some acquaintance with the principles and goals of its work. This is helped by regular opportunities for mutual discussion between all who are taking part in the expanded "team work."

As we consider the number and variety of people who may have an essential part in this many sided work of marriage counseling it seems clear that it is not a specialized branch of any profession or calling, but rather a specialized branch of counseling: an attitude and method of helping troubled people that is being more and more widely used by all the professions and by a steadily increasing number of trained laymen.

2. THE SPECIAL ASSETS AND PROBLEMS OF MINISTERS IN MARRIAGE COUNSELING

Whatever may be thought by the minister or anyone else about his fitness or otherwise for marriage counseling, in actual fact he is generally quite unable to escape some responsibility for it, because people will come to him for help in their marital troubles, and because ministers are found in many small towns and isolated places where trained marriage counselors are not easily available.

Apart from his geographical availability one of the greatest assets of the minister in marriage counseling is the fact that in his pastoral visiting and general pastoral care of his people he will often have a better opportunity than anyone, except possibly the family doctor, to discover and deal with many

marital stresses and conflicts at an early stage, often long before the partners would have taken the necessary initiative
to seek proper help. In this way a minister can do a great deal
of creative work in the healing of marital disorders before
they grow to serious enough proportions to reach the marriage counselor. This is quiet and unobtrusive work, which
could be still better if all ministers were given more training
in marriage counseling as an essential part of their theological
course.

Another asset of the minister is that in many cases he already
has the confidence of both partners, especially if he has
watched them grow up, and has prepared and married them,
and as long as he has shown himself to be a man of discretion
and understanding who is not prone to gossip. He also has
the privilege of calling on people on his own initiative.

In himself also the minister will generally have the spiritual
awareness and sense of vocation which are valuable in any
such "helping" activity, and which give power to his pastoral
attitude and skill. He may also have behind him a strong and
warm Christian Church fellowship, from which reunited
couples may draw much further strength, and to which they
may give grateful creative service, and deepen their own
union in so doing.

Professionally the minister has an important asset for marriage counseling by virtue of the conviction that economic,
sexual, personal, parental and social adjustments between marriage partners can only be adequately achieved when they are
woven into a relationship which is basically spiritual, whether
they realize it clearly or not. As long as this is offered in un-
derstandable terms to partners and not obscured behind words
which may not have meaning to them, the minister can offer
the central factor in all personal relationships to counselors
with whom he comes into contact, as well as to his parishioners.

Alongside these and similar assets of the minister there are some special problems implicit in his position. One of these is time. He has a special responsibility to the whole body of people committed to his care, and specific duties which need careful and time consuming preparation apart from the hours involved in their performance. He has the difficult task of allotting his all too little available time between many conflicting claims on it. The same applies to his energies. This would seem to be something worthy of considerable discussion by groups of ministers, so that their whole scale of vocational priorities can be reviewed in the light of present day needs and demands. Many ministers agree that it is impossible to give more than about twelve hours per week to counseling in general without detriment to their total work.

Another special vocational problem of the minister in marriage—(and also in individual) counseling is found in his relationship with people apart from the counseling. This may have several consequences. In the first place however genuine his "unshockability" may be, clients may not feel free to discuss some elements of their difficulties as well with him as with a "secular" counselor. Even if they do manage to talk out many deeper feelings they may then come to feel some difficulty and possible embarrassment when they have to face him later in the pastoral relationship. The secular counselor is free from this difficulty in that his clients do not have to face him again unless by their own desire. However much the minister accepts what he is told in non-judgmental fashion, people will still cast him all too often into the role of judge, and that may hinder his approach to the deeper elements of the counseling.

Apart from the role into which other people may cast the minister he has a few conflicting roles of his own to sort out. One of these conflicts is between the essential moralism of his preaching and his personal example and convictions, and on the other hand the necessary permissiveness of counseling relationships. A possible clue to the way through such a conflict is in the example of Jesus, who represented and proclaimed the "straight and narrow way" but at the same time could be permissive enough to invite Himself to dine with Zaccheus, to eat with "publicans and sinners," and to refrain from condemnation of a woman "in adultery." Permissiveness has to be seen as distinct from condoning, and it has been found quite possible to reconcile this apparent inconsistency by very many ministers in their pastoral care of their people and any who may seek their help.

Another of these conflicts is between the minister's training and his popularly accepted role as someone who talks on all kinds of subjects and on all kinds of occasions on the one hand, and his counseling role as listener on the other. It is difficult for many ministers, and indeed for many other professional people, to switch from talking to listening, but it has to be done if the counseling is to succeed.

Perhaps the most difficult of all problems for the minister, reverting to the question of time and energy, is that the more successful he is in any counseling work the more demands will be made on his time and energy and the more trouble he will have in allotting it. It is generally harder for the minister to decline an invitation or application for help from someone in deep distress than it is for members of most other professions, but if the minister is to keep his spiritual vitality and his efficiency as well as to do justice to his domestic responsibilities, he has to learn to delegate what can be delegated to other people, and to allot his time and energy wisely with the courage of his own convictions. In some cases he may need counseling himself in order to come adequately to grips with this problem through the disentangling of his own inner feelings and conflicts.

It is becoming more widely realized that the minister's training should include some adequate opportunities for submission of himself for counseling as well as the practical and the theological elements which are now generally accepted as essential. When this is done there will be a great enrichment of the whole personal influence of ministers in any community, and particularly in the fields of marriage counseling and general pastoral counseling.

3. THE SPECIAL ASSETS AND PROBLEMS OF DOCTORS IN MARRIAGE COUNSELING

By setting themselves up in private practice or accepting salaried positions in institutions and public services, doctors undertake to help those who come under their care in general or limited fields to the extent of at least reasonable competence. Apart from their actual medical responsibilities they are expected as educated, trained and respected citizens to exert a positive influence in the community.

Whatever their ideas about marriage counseling it is as true of doctors as of ministers that they cannot avoid contact with marital disorders, or the social and professional obligation to do what they can to help in their resolution.

Many marital disorders come direct to a doctor in the first place, because the partners find him most easily accessible, and regard him as the most logical person from whom to seek advice and help. It may be a direct marital squabble which is distressing one or both to the point at which they feel the need of medical help, or even someone to talk to about it. It may go further, and one partner who has been attacked may come or be brought to a doctor for attention, or for the recording of cuts and bruises for possible litigation later. It may be that one or both partners are seeking help and advice with regard to some kind of sexual dissatisfaction or difficulty, or some apparent abnormality. A special example of this is when a wife returns home after giving birth to her first or a subsequent baby and finds herself indifferent to the sexual relationship with her husband, who has patiently waited through the final months of her pregnancy for it.

Other direct points of medical contact with marital disorders may be for such questions as family planning, especially at the time of marriage and after the first or a subsequent child, and in some cases there are differences and conflicts about this. Or there may be direct quarrels about the management of children and the doctor may be appealed to as an "umpire." Or again there may be deep and growing suspicions by one partner about the fidelity of the other, and the doctor may be appealed to either for help in standing up to such threats, or for moral support when there seems nobody else to talk to.

There are also many indirect ways in which a doctor may come into contact with a marital conflict. Especially if the doctor is young and not well established people will often hesitate about telling him directly of their marital troubles, but may come ostensibly for help with some apparently unrelated symptom which arises from the marital disorder. For example the complaint may be of tiredness, nervousness, lack of sleep, restlessness, and the desire for a tonic, or some such nervous symptom. Or it may show itself as a "psychosomatic disorder," such as indigestion, colitis, asthma, migraine, or certain kinds of dermatitis. In women there may be some gynecological symptom.

In more severe or prolonged cases the presenting problem may be some neurotic or even apparently psychotic manifestation, which may even reach the point of attempted suicide, either from despair or as an attempt to "punish" the partner. Of course marital disorder is not one of the fundamental causative factors of such mental illness, but it may well prove to be an influential precipitating factor, or may greatly intensify such troubles or hinder their recovery. As such it comes right into the field of medical practice.

A still less direct, but very important method of medical contact with marital disorder, may come through a third person, particularly through some trouble affecting one or more of the children. Poor health in a child without any obvious reason may open up inquiries by the doctor about the domestic atmosphere, particularly if the child is becoming increasingly nervous or "difficult." The situation between the parents may be revealed on the other hand when a child or adolescent shows some consequence of parental neglect or mismanagement, such as when a teen-age girl is brought to the doctor for a pre-marital pregnancy, or a boy finds himself with prospective paternal responsibilities without benefit of marriage. Or a teen-age boy or girl may have been the cause of a serious or fatal accident because of some careless and irresponsible escapade. There are all kinds of different ways in which the doctor may come into contact with marital disorder if he is awake to the possibility and ready to look into underlying causes.

It still happens all too frequently that a doctor faced with one or more of the symptoms or indirect consequences of marital disorder tends to leave the underlying causes untouched and to tell his patient that the trouble is with his "nerves" or that he "can't find anything physically wrong." Such a statement should be the beginning of positive investigation and therapy and not the end of it, and many opportunities of helping married people in troubles at a stage at which they are quite open to help are missed. With more general awareness of the influence of marital disorders on physical and emotional troubles, and more realization of the "curability" of many such marital disorders, this medical responsibility will be more often and more worthily fulfilled.

At this point it might be stated that there are many indications that a reasonable training in marriage counseling will not only improve the doctor's handling of marital disorders, but will make a very great difference to the whole of his handling of people, in whatever department of medicine his work and interest may lie.

Apart from his frequent contact with marital disorders the doctor has many valuable assets for marriage counseling. His education and training give him the capacity for looking behind symptoms to underlying causes, and for intelligent and reasoned assessment of the complex elements of problems. He gains experience with all kinds of people in situations through which he can see below the surface and understand many of their deeper feelings and motives. He knows their best and their worst qualities, and they feel better because he accepts them in spite of their less respectable selves.

People also know that the doctor will treat their revelations in the strictest confidence, and that helps them to come and to be open with him. They also feel freer to talk to him about matters which tend to be "taboo" in other conversation, such as the intimate sexual feelings and experiences; and they also know that he is equipped with resources by which they can gain some temporary relief from their distress and anxiety.

In addition they have confidence in his wisdom and judgment, and often an exaggerated confidence in the extent to which his statements and directions will be accepted and followed by others. They often appear to expect him to "convince" the marital partner of the enormity of what he is doing, as if the doctor were a super judge, but that does not seriously diminish his assets for counseling.

Yet another professional asset of the doctor is in the fact that people can seek his help without the same kind of admission of marital failure as would be involved in their going to a marriage counselor. When they feel hesitant to make any such open admission this may well be a crucial factor in the decision to seek help.

Finally it may be said that in many cases the doctor is honored by admission to the inner circle of his friendship and trust by many of his patients, and even if his help is not needed by them for marital trouble their warm recommendation and urgings will induce their friends who may be in trouble to go confidently for help to him.

Alongside these valuable assets the doctor has many problems in marriage counseling which are not always easy to overcome. The first of these is time. If he is a good doctor it is likely that there will be many demands on his available time and energy, and he will see the long and recurring interviews with people in marital trouble as beyond his power from that point of view. Unless he sets out as a professional service to do such work he will generally feel compelled to refer any but the simplest of such cases to a marriage counselor. But there is still much that he can do without undue expenditure of time. It has been found by many doctors that a good training in marriage and family counseling has enabled them to use their normally available time with patients much more effectively, and that they can help many people in the earlier stages of marital disorder greatly without overspending their time and energy.

Another problem which may hinder the doctor from effectiveness in marriage counseling is his professional orientation. The surgeon, for example, or the specialist in some limited field, may feel that he has quite enough on his mind in dealing adequately with the physical condition of his patient and keeping up with the details of his chosen field. He may feel unable to devote time or energy to any marital difficulties which may underlie or be associated with the trouble. He will generally be glad to hand over this part of the situation to someone else.

The gynecologist may deal with marital problems mainly if not entirely from the limited area surrounding any structural or functional disorders in the reproductive organs of women, and as an interested doctor he may allow himself to be drawn to some extent into the associated emotional conflicts for the purpose of helping in their resolution. But his special abilities in the more limited field are of most value in the role of consultant, where he may give invaluable service to troubled women, particularly in matters concerning apparent infertility.

The pediatrician may sometimes be drawn into marital disorders through his work with sick children, but here again, unless he has a special interest and sense of vocation for helping to deal with the disordered relationship between the partners, he will be glad to hand that aspect of the problem over to someone else.

The physician who takes the trouble to assess the deeper factors behind many so-called "stress diseases" which come under his care will inevitably be drawn into many marital disorders, which are often playing such an influential part in the trouble that no great relief will come until the marital situation has been relieved to some appreciable extent. Many physicians have an interest and considerable aptitude in dealing with the emotional factors behind the symptoms and signs of people, and do a lot of effective marriage counseling in the course of their work.

Psychiatrists are probably doing more marriage counseling than any other kind of medical specialist, because many of the troubled people who come to them for help either have marital troubles as one of the causative factors or else develop them as a consequence of their illness. As we have seen, the psychiatrist's main field of work is in the intra-personality field, but he is in no sense limited to that. With the development of psychiatry its scope is constantly being widened and matters concerning human relationships are inseparable from any psychiatrist's work.

There are two possible difficulties implicit in the psychiatrist's professional role as it affects marriage counseling, apart from the inevitable problem of time. One is that people in marital difficulty are often hesitant to seek help directly from a psychiatrist because they regard his main function as concerned with the abnormal, or with the mentally ill. He is thereby denied many opportunities of helping people in marital disorder at an early stage when they are more easily and quickly relieved. The cost of a long series of counseling sessions from a psychiatrist sometimes constitutes a decisive factor in making people try to do without his help in the hope that things will somehow improve. In many cases the psychiatrist will come into contact with marital disorder through referral by a family doctor.

Another difficulty implicit in the professional orientation of the psychiatrist as it affects marriage counseling is that his work and his thinking are mainly in the intra-personal field. This is especially true of the psychoanalysts, and those who work mainly in psychotherapy with individual patients often find it necessary to reorient themselves considerably when faced with a problem which is mainly (though not generally exclusively) in the relationship field. Freudian analysts insist that a separate therapist should deal with each partner in any situation in which they both seek help, while marriage counselors take the view that they can help much more when the same counselor deals with both partners. It may be that the growing practice of "group psychotherapy" will lead to some reconciliation of these two different points of view, and that the psychotherapists will move further into the relationship area than many of them have felt able to do as yet.

The psychiatrist is an absolutely necessary resource for marriage counselors as a consultant, as is made clear in many parts of this book. With the inadequate numbers of available psychiatrists it may be that the most efficient use that can be made of them by the community in marriage disorders will be in the role of consultants.

The general practitioner is another member of the medical profession who comes into contact with very many cases of marital disorder. Either he or the minister is generally the first person, after the relatives, to be consulted. Many general practitioners do a large amount of effective counseling in marriage disorders and in all kinds of other situations, and develop considerable practical skill and experience in doing it. But the main problems here are again those of time and of difficulties in keeping up sufficient study in the extraordinarily diverse requirements of his professional role. Unfortunately the training of most doctors does not include any real teaching or practice in matters concerning the marital relationship or in counseling in most medical schools, and even with all the difficulties of an overfull curriculum it would seem that the time is ripe for this to be carefully reconsidered.

4. THE SPECIAL ASSETS AND PROBLEMS OF MEMBERS OF OTHER PROFESSIONS

Social workers, and particularly psychiatric social workers, have a training and experience which can be of the greatest value in marriage counseling. Their awareness of the inner dynamics of personal attitude and behavior, their training in case work, and their experience with people in all kinds of "stress situations" constitute a basic foundation for marriage counseling which is probably as strong as that of any profession. When they build on to this foundation a specific study and training in matters concerning the marital relationship and its disorders they are probably better equipped in the all round competence for marriage counseling than any other profession.

But their main problems, as with other professions, are concerned with the allotment of time and energy, and with the professional orientation which is predominantly focussed on the social environmental aspects of distress, though not by any means excluding the relational aspects or even the intrapersonal. As members of the staff of many social agencies and psychiatric clinics, social workers are doing some very effective service in marriage and family counseling, and they will tend to do more and more as the needs become more accepted in the public mind. They can offer quite distinctive assistance in the team work of any marriage counseling agency, and their expert knowledge of the social aspects of marital disorder is of great help in the training of marriage counselors as well as in the actual professional work of counseling.

Clinical psychologists also have many assets which are of great use in marriage counseling, particularly their experience in assessing personality characteristics by objective testing and their understanding of the inner dynamics of personal attitude and behavior. In countries where marriage counseling is predominantly carried on by university graduates there is always a large percentage of trained psychologists in the field, who have supplemented their professional training with some special training and experience in marriage counseling and related concerns. As members of a counseling team and as consultants where their special competence is needed they form an indispensable part of the whole undertaking.

Lawyers cannot escape contact with many marital disorders, and their attitude seems to vary from that of doing everything possible to open the dispute to counseling to that of simply giving advice and being willing to act for the person who may wish to seek the dissolution of a marriage. Their vocational aptitude and training give them many valuable assets for counseling; clear orderly minds, ability to think into situations and to sift the significant from the inapplicable, and the knowledge of the law as it affects the various questions that may arise. But the lawyer cannot generally afford the time necessary for any serious counseling, nor has he the training in the actual work of counseling. He is an adviser and clarifier rather than a therapist. He is an indispensable resource for consultation to save distressed people from actions which may increase rather than diminish their difficulties, and sometimes to make it clear to a misbehaving partner that if he persists in his actions he can be challenged in court.

Probation officers are also brought into contact with many marital disorders in their work, and are doing much quiet work in helping people to work through marital difficulties. Their training would appear at present to be generally insufficient for serious marriage counseling, but many of them develop a good practical competence in the course of their careers. They are responsible to the courts, and this may sometimes reduce their professional freedom in marriage counseling, and may possibly deter some couples from allowing them to know the inner elements of the marital trouble. But probation officers are valuable people to have available in many special cases, often cases of considerable difficulty.

Teachers also come into contact with marital disorders, mainly through such offenses by children as truancy, vandalism, and other behavior problems. Sometimes the beginning of the teacher's acquaintance with a marital disorder is when a child who has been doing well in class suddenly begins to do badly and to slip downward toward the bottom of the class. Where school term reports are the rule the parents will often seek some explanation of the change, and the teacher may be able to help them to realize the connection between emotional strain and poor school work. While teachers are professionally oriented mainly in the direction of education rather than therapy, there is a welcome movement in educational circles toward the concern about the emotional aspects of learning and growth. The teacher with a strong vocational sense and an interest in the total personality and the family backgrounds of his pupils can be of great help in such matters as marriage counseling.

It is likely, however, that there will be an even greater development and use of teachers in the future in the work of education and preparation for marriage than there has ever been in the past. This important work needs to be carried out wherever young people are, in small towns and villages as well as large cities, and the leadership in the future would seem to be in the combined hands of the doctor, the minister and the teacher, the three most suitable professional people for the work who can be found in the smallest villages as well as the large cities.

This consideration of the special assets and problems of the various professional workers seems to point to the conclusion that marriage counseling must be mainly in the hands of suitable people who have undertaken special training for it and are able and willing to give the necessary time and concentration to it. But there is a first-class field of service for other people as we have seen, who can help people in marital trouble as part of their own professional service, and in many cases can be used as consultants in their own special fields.

This consideration leads inevitably to the more detailed survey of the necessary personal qualities in the counselor as affecting the work of marriage counseling. This question will now be discussed.

5. THE PERSONALITY AND THE ATTITUDES
OF THE MARRIAGE COUNSELOR

We have discussed the different "kinds" of people who might be involved in marriage counseling, and mentioned some of the personal and professional qualities that are generally required for the work. It is the universal experience that the quality of the counselor's own personality is the most influential factor in any form of genuine counseling, and it is therefore of some value to consider and to try to formulate the most desirable qualities of personality and the most helpful attitudes of the counselor in counseling.

We may remind ourselves at the beginning that interviewing and counseling are, or should be, reciprocal relationships between two people "for the benefit of one." Counselor and client will each have their share of the universal endowment of conscious and repressed feelings; of prejudices, vulnerabilities, uncritical assumptions about life and about people, habitual attitudes and emotional needs. Any of these may be stirred up in the emotional interaction inseparable from counseling. Unless the counselor has some awareness of his own inner qualities and vulnerabilities and a reasonable control of them, his own emotional reactions may well intrude into the counseling relationship to such an extent and intensity as to ruin the counseling.

Many people are attracted to counseling for quite unworthy reasons, of which they are mostly unaware. In some cases they have a deep need to assert themselves, to control other people's lives and destinies, and in this and other ways to satisfy a "will to power," as Adler called it. Others may be anxious about prestige and status more than they realize, and not really open to the needs of others. Others again are over-curious, and seem to gain some kind of satisfaction in hearing about the intimate details of people's private lives. Others again have deep suppressed hostilities which all too easily become projected onto a "helpless" client who unwittingly touches a vulnerable part of the counselor's personality. Others again are seeking flattery and adulation, and tend to be over-ingratiating in the counseling, and some are openly seductive, with a deep need to induce clients to "fall" for them. It is obvious that any such qualities will do much more harm than good to the whole project of counseling, and may induce an inept counselor to reverse the whole aim of the counseling and use the client for the counselor's benefit or satisfaction.

These and similar underlying distortions of personality are not generally realized by those in whom they exist, and who may well offer themselves for the work of counseling. Fortunately such qualities can often become obvious to a competent counselor or psychiatrist in an introductory interview or series of interviews, or to many other people when they have fairly close contact with the person in a discussion group or week-end conference in which they live together. Such methods are therefore generally adopted as part of a good "selection" procedure. A good description of the present selection procedure in Great Britain for prospective counseling trainees is given by J. H. Wallis in "Marriage Counseling," by J. H. Wallis and H. S. Booker (Routledge and Kegan Paul, London, 1958) pages 45-56, and an account of their training is given in the same book, pages 57-73.

Among the many personal qualities that are generally sought in the initial selection of prospective marriage counselors are the following:

1. Honesty, integrity of character, trustworthiness and ability to hold communications in strict confidence.

2. An open mind and a liberal and tolerant outlook, free

from restrictive prejudice and not prone to take sides in personal conflicts.

3. Emotional and personal balance and poise, with flexibility in attitude and practice; awareness of own limitations as well as abilities and powers.

4. Clear insight and capacity for reasoned analysis; and ability to visualize the importance of deeper elements in personal and social problems.

5. Ability to discuss intimate and emotionally charged matters without embarrassment.

6. Acceptance of and loyalty to the aims of the Marriage Guidance or Counseling organization.

7. Deep and genuine warmth and "non-exploitative" interest in people, without personal involvement or "vested interest" in results of counseling. Readiness to go with partners even through break-up of their marriage if they decide to do so.

8. Capacity to be a good listener, easy to talk to when one is in trouble, and able to inspire and win the confidence of all kinds of people of both sexes and different ages.

9. Genuine patience, not too impulsive with the offering of "solutions," or eager to give answers or reassurances, and yet able to offer constructive help as well as understanding.

10. Persistence with which to see a difficult case through.

11. Permissiveness and non-judgmental objectivity, without disguising personal standards and values or seeking to impose them on others.

12. Reasonable freedom from unsolved personal and marital problems, and reasonable awareness of emotional needs.

It is clear that in any preliminary selection these qualities of personal character and relationship must be regarded more as guides than as absolute standards, or there would probably be very few candidates for training as counselors. Many of these qualities are found to be developed to a considerable extent in any good course of training, and they are further stimulated in the actual work of counseling. No matter how many of these qualities any counselor may have, he will always find room for further growth and development.

Beyond these personal qualities there are many "vocational" and "technical" abilities which are mainly achieved in the training courses and further developed throughout all active counseling work, through contact with people in need of help, experience of actual counseling, and through team work, professional supervision, consultations, and case discussions over the years of service.

The good counselor then will have a genuine readiness to look at each problem that comes to him through each partner's eyes, not to judge or to give advice or superficial reassurance, but to go with each of them right down into the agonizing bewildering situation and into their background ideas, attitudes and emotional needs. Then he will patiently support them while they are relating these to the realities of their marital relationship and making the necessary modifications in application of their new insights and their liberated feelings.

CHAPTER IV

The General Setting of Marriage Counseling

I. WHERE SHOULD MARRIAGE COUNSELING TAKE PLACE?

IT SEEMS INEVITABLE—when marriage counseling may be performed by such a variety of people, informally as well as formally—that it will be carried on in various kinds of locations, but some principles that seem worthy of emphasis bear on the "geographical" aspect of the work.

When marriage counseling is carried on through a voluntary social or professional organization it is generally regarded as essential that all such work should be done at the official headquarters of the organization. Matters of crucial importance, such as the comprehensive team work and the necessary supervision together with the absolute necessity of keeping all case records and other documents strictly confidential and under lock and key, can only be safeguarded in this way. It is also an important part of the necessary counseling relationship that it should be left to clients to take the initiative in actually coming and seeking help rather than just allowing the help to come to them. There are many other valid reasons why marriage counseling at the homes of clients is inadvisable, except in very special cases when it may be absolutely unavoidable.

Many social and religious organizations offer a marriage counseling service as part of their contribution to the community welfare, and this again, for the same reasons, is generally carried on at the headquarters of the particular organization.

Private professional marriage counseling by psychiatrists, physicians, psychologists, social workers and others, is again generally carried on in the practitioner's consulting rooms, whether it is accepted as an exclusive activity or is included in a more varied and wider professional range. The same principles and reasons apply to this as to the more organized marriage counseling.

Ministers of religion cannot escape frequent requests for help in marital disorders, and some ministers become very competent in marriage counseling. Here again, however plausible and urgent any requests may be for counseling of this kind in the parishioner's home it seems much better in general for it to be done in the minister's own study, which throws the initiative onto the client. In a disturbed marital relationship there is always some deep emotional involvement, and the fact that a minister, or any other kind of counselor, calls repeatedly at the home of a wife who is estranged in any way from her husband, may well bring about deep and serious misunderstandings not likely to be helpful to the particular case or to the professional standing of the counselor.

Lawyers would seem in most if not all cases to perform the function of attempted reconciliation of estranged partners in their professional chambers, and when any divorce court judge decides to see the partners with a view to reconciliation he would naturally do so in his own chambers.

Lastly it may be emphasized that the place to which clients go for marriage counseling should be as unobtrusive as well as reasonably accessible as possible. People do not wish it to

be obvious that they are visiting a marriage guidance or counseling agency.

2. THE PRELIMINARIES OF MARRIAGE COUNSELING

The initial act which sets the whole process of marriage
counseling in motion is usually the making of an appointment
by one or both of the partners, or sometimes by someone in
their behalf. This is usually done by telephone or by letter, or
by direct personal visit to the agency, clinic, or professional
rooms. It is generally agreed that in all cases of trouble or
illness in which emotions are involved, the "helping" process
begins with the first contact with the chosen source of help,
and is assisted or hindered by the attitudes and actions of
everyone who may be concerned in the work.

The person who answers the telephone, the door of the
agency or consulting rooms, and any letters that are written,
may have a vital influence on the whole course of the helping
process. A natural, warm, friendly interest and an intuitive grasp
of the feelings of people, with a genuine attempt to meet
their needs as well as possible, will do much to start the
work on the right foot.

The emotional "climate" of any agency or consulting rooms
will depend partly on wise choice of staff, but possibly even
more on the kind of relationship that exists between all who
work together, from the director to the most junior helper.
When the team work is of good quality, and the members
have regular opportunities for keeping together, the nature of
the work itself will help to promote good fellowship. It
may be that such a simple occasion as a regular tea or coffee
break to which every member of the staff is welcomed, will
prove to be one of the best opportunities for such fellowship.

There is need for some flexibility with regard to appointment times to allow the more urgent cases to be attended to

without undue delay, but this of course depends on the relationship between the demands for help and the available staff. It is of great help to the receptionist or to whomever makes the appointments to have some available time for urgent cases, and thus avoid the difficulty of having to involve them in distressing and possibly dangerous delay.

At the first appearance of any client or clients at an agency or clinic it is likely that some details will be recorded, such as names and addresses, telephone numbers (with information as to whether it is desired that the number should not be called at any given times), and possibly some other facts such as date and place (church or registry office) of marriage, any previous marriages and how they were terminated, age and sex of children, religious persuasion of husband and wife, active or nominal, and whether changed after marriage, and occupations of husband and wife. The source of referral is also generally recorded at this time, and the present state of the marriage (if broken, who left and when?).

These basic details may be obtained either by questioning of the client by the receptionist; or if more suitable to the organization, by the counselor; or they may be recorded by the clients on a special form before they begin the actual counseling. In some marriage counseling agencies the clients fill in a very extensive formal questionnaire, and thus provide full data for research purposes, with very careful safeguards against breach of confidence through keeping names and addresses separate from any copies of data used for research.

The advantage of recording of data by the receptionist or by the clients before counseling is that the counselor will not have to risk leading the client to believe that he is looking mainly for factual data when he really is most concerned about the feelings of the client, and about what the facts or the experiences mean to the client. It also helps to make sure that these data will be recorded. On the other hand, when the counselor records these basic data his doing so will sometimes give the client a good opportunity to collect his or her thoughts, and "feel" his way into the counseling situation while giving these routine facts. The counselor can easily make it clear then that he is interested in how the client feels by his responses to any feelings that are expressed in the narrative.

The whole question of recording of interviews by the counselor is of some importance. From the client's point of view it is probably best if, after taking down the essential preliminary data, the counselor can put down his pen and give his full and undivided attention to the client; but in some cases this may have the drawback that the counselor will have to depend on his memory for the main details. When one counselor is dealing with a fairly large number of clients, this will obviously be very difficult. It may be possible for the counselor to write down a fairly full account of the interview immediately after it has been terminated, and with practice this may give a better record than anything written down during the interview. For any counselor it is most valuable to have a record of the main details of each interview, because he is then able to refresh his memory just before each subsequent interview and begin it with some awareness of the client's previous feelings and experiences. This makes for much better rapport, and much greater efficiency.

Another alternative is for the client or the counselor to record a fuller range of data, including possibly some of the complaints and experiences of each client during the interviews, and then for the counselor to make his own record of the appropriate details at the end of the sessions after the client has departed.

In some training centers in different parts of the world tape recordings of interviews are made, with the permission of the client and with safeguards against breach of confidence. This is of great value for the training of new counselors, with no disclosure of names, and also for the continuing training of established counselors. Such recordings can be the only means of checking the actual quality of the work of any counselor, and may well help a counselor to check his own attitudes and methods. So far it has not been used in marriage counseling centers in Australia, but it seems essential that some such method of improving and safeguarding the standards of this work will need to be considered and organized.

In some American training schools selected interviews are carried out in rooms equipped with special windows which allow observation in one direction only, so that trainees can see and hear (through headphones) the whole interview, without knowing the name of the client. This is another excellent manner by which people can be trained for the very skilled work of marriage counseling, and by which the whole quality of the work can be improved.

3. WHAT SHOULD BE INCLUDED IN THE RECORDS OF MARRIAGE COUNSELING?

If we are to gain further specific knowledge from the rapidly growing and developing work of marriage counseling it is essential that reliable and reasonably comprehensive records should be kept, and that they should be kept in such a manner that any use of them will be for general statistical purposes and with absolute safeguard of the confidential nature of all that is disclosed to any marriage counselor. This safeguarding is generally carried out by distinguishing all records by a number and keeping the corresponding names and addresses on a separate cross-indexed file under lock and key, as of course are the records themselves.

It is important for the value of the records and also for

the counselor's own orderly thinking and learning that he should keep at the back of his mind a fairly comprehensive picture of the main details which need to be recorded. In this way he is less likely to overlook some important aspect of the trouble which the partners may not volunteer to him in the course of the interviews, but which they will readily discuss if he asks a suitable "creative question" at the right time.

Much of the necessary material will be discussed later in this book but a brief summary at this point of the main headings under which the records may be made will possibly help the counselor to build up a simple and easily remembered picture of what is valuable in the records.

The basic routine details of names, addresses, ages, religious affiliations, and other similar matters are for each counseling agency to decide upon in its standard record sheet, and these are often recorded at the time of registration by the receptionist, although there is no reason why the counselor should not record them if that seems more workable. But the counselor will help in future research if he sees that clear records are made of some specific matters at least, and these can be divided for convenience into seven groups of data:—Observation of the clients, Clients' motives for coming, Present situation, Clients' feelings about the difficulty, Previous history, Counselor's assessments, and Final Outcome and Follow-up.

a. *Observation of the clients.* This is a useful beginning of each consecutive record, and it is most often neglected. It may include such characteristics as the following:—

Appearance:—strained, anxious, restless, "on guard," indifferent, despairing, or hostile.

Dress:—neat or careless, restrained or flamboyant, etc.

Manner and behavior:—weeping, aggressive, withdrawn,

clinging, or seductive, able to look counselor in the face, hand movements.

Speech:—voluble or reticent or silent, coherent or rambling, repetitive, restrained or hostile and aggressive.

The change in the records of the clients' appearance with the progress of counseling may offer a very good indication of what is happening, one which may not be so obvious from the record of what the clients say. Such records also offer an extra dimension by which the client can be pictured in the mind of the counselor in reviewing his case history, and by anyone doing research in the counseling field.

b. *The clients' main motives for coming.* Did they come willingly on their own initiative, or in the case of the second client in willing response to a letter of invitation by the counselor? Were they easily persuaded to come by a friend or relative, or referred by a minister, doctor, lawyer, or other person? Did they come rather hesitantly because of an appeal by someone to "give it just one more chance?" Or were they directed to come by a divorce court judge, and if so was it because they hadn't realized the availability of counselors or in spite of their own indifference or rebellious hostility? These are important details which may easily be omitted from the counselor's records unless he keeps them specifically in mind and develops good habits of recording.

As a corollary to the actual expressed motives for coming the counselor may gain some idea from the statements of the clients of their expectations from the counseling. Did they believe that the counselor would listen to them and ask any questions and then give his judgment and advice? Did they think it would only need one interview? These expectations are better picked up in the actual discussion, especially when the counselor comes to the point of defining the counseling situation and its goals; rather than made the subject of actual questions, at least at the beginning.

c. *The present situation, as seen by the clients, and in their own words.* Are they living together at the present time, if not how and when did they separate? If together what degree of tension? Can they communicate? How did the trouble develop and from when? Any events or experiences which seem to have helped to bring it about? How long married? What children—age, sex, temperament? Illnesses, living conditions, Jobs, Neighborhood, How do they relate in sex, personally, socially, parentally? What seem to be the main points of discord or vulnerability?

d. *The clients' feelings about their difficulties and about themselves and each other.* This is put in a separate heading to emphasize the need for recording of feelings as well as facts. Many records of less experienced counselors are almost entirely limited to the facts of the dispute and give no idea of how either client felt about them. With this account there may be information about each client's feelings about the "in-laws," about children, jobs, habits and all kinds of other matters which may stir up feelings.

Behind these feelings the counselor will try to evaluate each partner's "role perceptions" and "role expectations" in marriage and parenthood, and any consequent feelings of "role frustration." Behind these again he may discern some patterns of habitual attitudes and emotional needs and uncritical assumptions, all of which will be dealt with later. They are essential elements in a good record.

e. *Previous history of each partner,* as seen, if possible by both separately. Such matters as family background, school and social life, introduction to sex, courtship, previous engagements or marriages and how terminated and with what feelings, and any other relevant matters. By hearing how each client views his partner's family and other history as well as his own it is possible to gain a two-dimensional appreciation of the background "conditioning" of each of them, as we have seen in the case of John and Mary at the beginning of this book.

f. *The counselor's assessment* at the end of each interview, and an evaluation of the apparent development of the clients' insight and the matters which seem to be still in need of discussion, form a good progress report, and a help in the re-establishment of rapport in the next interview. Such records also give a valuable unfolding picture of the progress of the counselings, from which the counselor can learn much about his own counseling attitudes.

g. *Final outcome, and (if possible) follow-up.* This is mainly an assessment of the counselor's general impressions after the apparently final interview, and it gives him and any supervisor a good opportunity to sum up his conduct of the whole case. Some agencies write to their clients at intervals to ask them how their marriage has worked out, and any such information which can be obtained is valuable. It is not certain whether such communications are favored by clients in all cases, but with some such plan of follow-up inquiries adopted by any agency it is possible to prepare for it during the counseling by asking clients whether they would like such a regular communication. In most cases it would be welcomed when put that way, and in fact many happy clients write spontaneously to their counselor, sometimes at Christmas, telling of their happiness and harmony and any other homely matters that occur to them. But such communications do not constitute a reliable sample for research purposes because the unsatisfactory cases are not likely to write in this way.

Another use for such comprehensive records is in cases when

after one or two interviews the clients fail to come again. It is of some value to know the reason for this as far as possible, and some ideas may well be gained from the record and from the counselor's recollection of the kind and degree of rapport. In some cases the client or clients come to investigate the possibilities of getting emotional support or of getting the counselor to judge the situation or condemn the partner. When these and other unfulfillable aims are in clients' minds they may be so disappointed that they will not return, and the counselor has not time to win their confidence in such a way as to be able to define the normal aims of counseling.

In other cases partners may have found enough insights from the first interview to feel able to work out their relationship for themselves, even though the counselor may not have felt that the situation had advanced to any extent. This has occasionally been communicated to the counselor on a subsequent occasion, and he finds that he has achieved more than he knew.

When any client terminates the counseling in this way without any explanation it is a good thing for the counselor to review his conduct of the interview or interviews, and to recall his own feelings as he faced the client. Many such terminations arise from a feeling of rejection of some kind in the client, which he is unable to express except by staying away. In some such cases he will go to another counselor, and these feelings may then be expressed to the new counselor.

Finally a comprehensive record is of the greatest value in the necessary supervision of the work of less experienced counselors as part of their "in-service" training, and for their accreditation when that is required. It is also of value for case conferences through which again the whole work of counseling is greatly developed and improved, to the benefit of all future clients.

4. THE BACKGROUND AND THE FEELINGS OF
THE PARTNER SEEKING COUNSELING

Here is Molly Jones, sitting in the waiting room, awaiting the signal to go in and meet the counselor for the first time. What might she be thinking about as she sits, possibly with mixed feelings as she faces what may be to her a painful ordeal?

There may be many memories intertwining with one another in her mind. The marriage itself, it seemed so right then, but how different now! "Was I too impulsive, carried away by the desire to be married, or proud of being wanted by an attractive man? Should I have seen through him then as I do now? Could I have realized how interfering his mother would be, and how much under her thumb he was?"

She may be going over the many disagreements and conflicts, the cruel remarks and misunderstandings, the physical cruelty alternating with indifference and neglect, the intolerable crudeness and disgusting nauseating alcoholic behavior, the slow death of her love in the face of repeated unwarranted hostility and the growth of distrust and hatred in its place.

There may be memories too of some well-meaning attempts by relatives to find a solution to the conflicts, and the sequences of hope and despair as the old habits reasserted themselves so soon. The most hopeful of all were the courageous efforts she and Jack had made to let bygones be bygones and start again on a better footing, how they each felt that they understood the other better and that they loved each other in spite of having "got off on the wrong foot," and how utterly despairing she felt when the same old "techniques" came up within a couple of weeks of their "reconciliation."

She may be recalling her visit to her solicitor, and the awful difficulty of deciding whether to "take the plunge" and leave Jack—and what about the two children if she did? They'd miss their Daddy, and he would probably insist on regular access to them, and that would only make them unsettled and upset. Then there was the visit to her minister who had no realization that things were so bad, but Jack would have nothing to do with him. And then his suggestion to look for help from the marriage counselor and her inability to believe that the counselor could do anything in such a difficult situation, especially as Jack still said he wouldn't have anything to do with any third party.

So here she is, with all her diffidence and anxiety about coming, with some worries about the possibility of disloyalty in telling a complete stranger about Jack, and about the possible repercussions that might come of it. Yet there is an aching desire for someone to be able to straighten out her bewilderment, and to stop her from thinking round and round in circles. Will the counselor understand, and what will he try to do about the hopeless looking situation? Can he get hold of Jack and do anything to make him see reason? How can she tell him so that she will not make a fool of herself by breaking down? What does he want to know? Will he take Jack's part because men so often think alike and stand up for one another.

There may be many other and possibly quite different thoughts and feelings, such as the desire to get out of the intolerable marital situation at any cost, there may be deep attraction and desire for someone else whom she can't get out of her thoughts, or she may have already left and got a job, and become adjusted to her "independence" and yet still have doubts about the welfare of the children.

In almost every case, however, one can assume that there will be deeply hurt pride, righteous indignation at the behavior of Jack and probably his parents too, bewilderment, disillusionment and cynicism, anxiety and despair, feelings of

failure and guilt, and often aversion and indifference or burn-
ing hatred.

It is well for the counselor to allow for such feelings behind
the apparent calmness of the person we have called Molly,
as she comes with some curiosity into the counseling room,
sits down, and collects her thoughts so that she can begin
her story.

When a husband happens to come first, his memories and
feelings may well be somewhat similar to those already mentioned, but in general it may be said that men are more re-
luctant and diffident about discussing their private marital
affairs with any third party, except possibly a close personal
friend. In many cases a husband will not make the initial approach unless he is rather desperate, or unless his wife has
actually left him. He may feel confident even then that she
will come back of her own accord before long when she has
recovered from the emotional tension. But when the weeks
go by and there is no sign of her return, or when she still
assures him that she will not return, he may then become willing to sink his "pride" and come for help. He will often say
then "I'll do anything to get her back, I didn't realize things
were as bad as that, or that she felt as bad as that."

When the husband and wife make the initial appointment
and come together it suggests a mutual willingness to look for
a way through their difficulties. Many couples who have the
same mutual willingness will come separately because they
know that this is how marriage counselors generally begin with
any marital problem, and they feel better able to discuss their
troubles at first without each other's presence.

In such "joint" appointments there may be less intense feeling between them, and a short interview with them together
will disclose any evidence of intense emotional conflict. The
counselor might then suggest that it might be found easier if

one or other waited outside for a time. If they are ready to comply with this and are in any doubt about which one should have first interview, the counselor might suggest that the partner who seems to have most reserved feelings or to have least to say would be the appropriate one for the first interview. If one of them finds it more difficult to arrange suitable times for appointments, that one would generally be the right one with whom to begin.

In all of this preliminary discussion the counselor is beginning to establish an accepting permissive relationship with the partners, which will do much to help them to feel free to unburden their feelings without undue reserve or inhibition. If the counselor has used his own knowledge and experience to allow for the many and mixed feelings and memories behind those who come for help it will make him more sensitive to any cautious beginnings of unburdening that either of them may offer him. This will encourage them to go on with confidence.

CHAPTER V

The Initial Interviews

The initial interview with each partner is of vital importance for the success or failure of the whole process of counseling, because it has a large part in creating the "rapport" between each partner and the counselor so essential for effective counseling. Each client, as we have seen, comes with very mixed, and often intense feelings, not only from the emotional strains of the marital situation, but also from the strains of seeking help from a third party. Each client will therefore be very sensitive to any failure on the part of the counselor to accept him and his feelings. If the client is skeptical about the ability of counseling to help he may well use any lack of acceptance as an excuse for refusing to come again. Any setback in the development of rapport may disturb his sensitive feelings, and will possibly drive him back into his shell to such an extent as to block the counseling process.

I. RAPPORT

As the whole counseling process depends on the establishment and maintenance of rapport some attention to this aspect of the counselor-client relationship is essential. The term rapport is borrowed from the French phrase "en rapport," which means "in harmony" or "in accord." It implies for the client a deepening sense of "at homeness," and a confidence in the counselor's ability and readiness to accept him as he is, with any failings, and to give his full concentrated attention to him and his problems and difficulties. This of course is implied in the term "inter-view"—i.e., *viewing between.*

Some of the foundations of rapport are established by the reputation of the counseling agency or of the private counselor, and by the kind of recommendation which induces the client or clients to come for help. The friendly atmosphere and genuine desire to arrange the most helpful appointment possible which may be shown by the receptionist, the person who answers the telephone or any letters, and any other members of the staff will also help greatly, especially when a client is nervous and apprehensive.

The main factors in the development of rapport, however, are the personality and the attitude of the counselor, and his total handling of the fluctuating interaction which goes on throughout the whole series of interviews. The client may feel it first as a natural simple sincerity, a spontaneous "warmth," and a genuine interest and desire to understand and to help. As the interview goes on the client will come to feel more and more clearly that he is accepted in a non-judgmental manner, so that any sense of humiliation at having to open up his life to another person is gradually replaced by a growing feeling that he can unburden even the worst things about himself without fear of being condemned or rejected. He will also come to realize that he can talk freely about sexual attitudes, and other subjects which are not so freely discussed in ordinary social conversation.

At the same time the client will begin to realize that some of his expectations about the counselor and about the interview will not be fulfilled. He may be disappointed because the counselor will not take his "side," or share his "righteous indignation" about the attitudes and actions of his partner or his "in-laws." This will sometimes disturb the rapport for a time, but the counselor is not setting out to establish "rapport at any price," and cannot allow himself to be the judge. But his acceptance of even the client's disappointment in him will gradually tend to overcome the client's doubts and misgivings.

It may actually provide the first real step towards more realistic thinking on the part of the client, which may be a necessary part of his growth from a kind of childish dependency that may have been an important factor in the marital conflict.

In some cases the client will react with intense hostility to the counselor's failure to take his side, and such exaggerated feelings are generally an expression of deep repressed childhood attitudes to some important person in the client's early life, generally a parent. This irrational attitude, and others of similar nature, are generally the re-enacting of such early attitudes, and are described under the term "transference." They happen much more frequently in deeper psychotherapy than in the more superficial counseling, and when accepted and handled adequately they form an important part of the healing process. This subject of transference will be discussed more fully in a later part of this section.

There are some other contributions which the counselor can make to the establishment and maintenance of rapport. The realization that everything the client says is kept in strictest confidence and not disclosed to anyone without permission is of great value to him as he comes to face things about which he does not feel at all happy. Also the fact that he does not have to face the counselor except by his own initiative and desire. This may not always be the case, for example when a minister acts as counselor to one or two of his own parishioners with whom he may have continuing pastoral relationship. This is dealt with more fully in the section relative to the minister's assets and his hindrances as a marriage counselor.

There are many factors which affect the quality of the rapport which are to be found in the client, and these deserve some consideration. In the first place the degree of motivation for coming will have a very profound effect. The client who only comes to please someone else and not from a genuine desire for constructive help will obviously need more delicate and sensitive handling for the establishment of rapport than will the client who is anxious for help and confident of the value of counseling as a channel of help. In some cases the second partner comes with considerable doubt and very much "on guard," wondering how much has been reported about him, and what the counselor may be thinking about him. It is interesting to watch the progressive relaxation of such people as they come to feel the counselor's non-critical acceptance.

An occasional handicap to the establishment of rapport is in the fact that the client has been referred by someone with whom he has built up a good relationship. Every attitude the counselor may show at the beginning may then be compared with those of the previous counselor, and it may need some patience and tact for the new rapport to build on the previous one. The necessary repetition of some of the more painful or irritating parts of the narrative already given to the previous counselor may be distasteful to the client, and this feeling needs to be realized and accepted by the new counselor—or consultant—even though it delays the counseling process to some extent.

When clients are actually directed to attend the counselor, for example by the courts, there may be still more difficulties in the establishment of rapport. If the counselor is not an officer of the court, or an "official" of any kind, but a private individual working under an oath of secrecy which applies even to the courts, the situation is more workable. Such clients may have failed to come on their own initiative simply from lack of awareness of the availability of this kind of counseling or through passivity, or procrastination, or they may have been indifferent, skeptical, or even actively hostile to counseling. They may have been determined to separate, even though the judge feels that there is some hope of possible reconciliation.

When clients come by direction in this way the helping attempt is called conciliation to distinguish it from counseling, which involves willing clients who come on their own initiative. In such directed cases the counselor has first to attempt to win sufficient confidence for them to become willing to make any effort to cooperate at all in the interviews. One of the first steps in this is to encourage the clients to express fully their feelings about being sent for conciliation in this way. The counselor's warm acceptance of such negative feelings, and the clients' growing realization that there will be no pressure put on them to stay together will do much to break down any hostility or to overcome any indifference or skepticism which they may have had. When this has come about the conciliation leads into normal counseling.

When these adverse feelings have been overcome the clients will have developed good rapport with the counselor, and it seems obvious that he is by far the most appropriate person with whom they should have the opportunity to go on in the counseling. To set apart some people as "conciliators" with the idea of transferring clients who come to accept further help to "counselors" would ignore or do violence to one of the most essential principles of counseling, the delicate relationship known as rapport. Those who are given the responsibility of conciliation should be the most experienced and highly trained and sensitive counselors obtainable, and they should be able to give all the time necessary for continued counseling where that is accepted by the clients.

Rapport, then, provides the essential framework in which all aspects of the counseling process can go on. It enables the clients to become progressively less inhibited and defensive, and to allow deeply "bottled up" feelings to come to the surface and be dealt with. It also allows the counselor to suggest many things for their consideration which might otherwise have been quite unacceptable to them. As we have seen it is not something fixed or constant, but something which has to be maintained as well as established, and if possible progressively deepened. Rapport always tends to fluctuate at the beginning, and at some points in the counseling process when the counselor may feel that there is not sufficient understanding by the clients as to what is being attempted, he may help greatly by pausing to define the aims and even the methods of the counseling.

In particular at the beginning of any subsequent interviews it may often be necessary for the counselor to set out to restore some of the rapport that is often lost during the period between the interviews for various reasons, such as the client's feeling that he has said more than he intended, the negative influence of well-meaning and sometimes "all-knowing" relatives and friends, or the attitudes of the marital partner. The first few minutes of all subsequent interviews are often very important for the improvement or lessening of the rapport.

2. THE GENERAL CONDUCT OF THE INITIAL INTERVIEW

The initial greeting by the counselor should be simple, natural and spontaneous, neither effusive on the one hand nor indifferent and detached on the other. The counselor then sets out to encourage the client to tell his story in his own words and his own way by showing an attitude of "creative listening," a readiness to listen with active keen interest and attention but not of over-curiosity.

Clients vary greatly in the amount of encouragement they may need. Some plunge without any hesitation into a veritable torrent of words and feelings which may go on without pause for most of the interview, and to which the counselor can only listen with as much concentration as possible. In some of these cases the narrative is direct and coherent, and the counselor quickly gains an accurate perception of many aspects of the complex problem. In others it is more or less disconnected and even incoherent, and the counselor has the difficult task of gaining a reasonable idea of the conflicting and distressing feelings which have so taken control of the client as to bring considerable confusion about the whole affair.

Other clients may need more direct encouragement to unburden their feelings and experiences. They may be reserved and diffident, suspicious or indifferent, helpless and despairing, antagonistic or hostile, rigid or prejudiced. Any initial encouragement should not be of such a kind as to give the client any feeling of being pushed, and for this the counselor needs to be able to accept any of these initial attitudes in the client without becoming anxious himself. This acceptance of the client's feelings, whatever they may be, and however they may be expressed, may be communicated to him either by a quiet nod of the head, an encouraging "mmhmm," or by a simple "accepting" type of comment, generally in questioning form.

For example if an extremely nervous diffident client begins with a prolonged silence, the counselor will probably sit quietly and patiently for a time, and then he might make some quiet accepting and understanding comment, such as, "You're finding it a bit difficult?" with the implied question, "is that it?" expressed by the inflection of his voice rather than by words. If there is still a long silence it may be right for the counselor to go on accepting this too. Some people find it very difficult and embarrassing to talk about such painful matters, and to find the right words to make themselves understood, and the counselor's acceptance will help to put them at their ease. If

the silence goes on to the point at which it may be embarrassing the client further, some such comment as the following
may be of help:—"I'm sorry, but I'm not sure what you're
feeling about this. Is it that you don't know quite where to
begin, or that things are in such a muddle that you can't think
for the moment?" This kind of comment, made slowly and
quietly, may enable the client to communicate these "para-
lyzing" feelings.

As the client becomes launched on the story the counselor
may help best by refraining from interruption until there is a
favorable opportunity for a comment, such as may be provided
by a reasonable pause in the narrative. In general his most important function at this stage is to encourage the client to
keep talking and to tell his story in his own way and his own
time within the limits of the counseling session. In this way
he may gain some idea of what the client regards as important,
and avoid the risk of missing some important "leads," or of
imposing his own ideas and attitudes on the counseling relationship.

As the client talks the counselor is given many facts. Many
feelings and attitudes are also communicated to him, by the
client's appearance and behavior as well as by his words and
the intonations and cadences of his speech. The counselor
sets out at this stage to catch as many as possible of the "under-
tones" of feeling as he allows the client to reveal himself
progressively in an atmosphere of growing confidence.

This confidence will be most quickly established when the
counselor can listen patiently and give the client a really good
attentive hearing. When there is a pause in the narrative the
counselor can help by making a simple brief "questioning"
comment which responds to the feelings that have been expressed or implied rather than the facts which have been communicated. This is possibly the most important principle of
this initial stage of the interview, and it also applies through-

out all interviews. It encourages the client to progressive unburdening of feelings rather than of a long and involved series
of facts. And it is essential to any understanding of the rationale
of counseling to realize that this unburdening of feelings is a
necessary condition for the client's later achievement of insight.

Such response to the expressed feelings rather than the facts
of the narrative will help the client to gain some idea of what
his part in the counseling is. Many clients are very uncertain
of what happens in a situation such as this, and are feeling
their way and trying to gain some light to relieve their confusion. If the counselor responded to the facts of the client's
story the client would naturally conclude that the counselor
was interested in and wanted all the facts that were available.
He would then in most cases continue the story by giving a
long and involved succession of facts, some of which might
well be quite irrelevant, because the client in his confusion
may not be able to arrange the large amount of material in
any kind of coherent manner. As fact follows fact the counselor may well find his brain beginning to reel with confusion
in the desperate attempt to take it all in and to arrange the
complicated story in some kind of order. He will then find
it very difficult to establish rapport with the client, because
rapport is mainly an emotional relationship.

In many cases, even when the counselor responds to the
client's feelings, there will be so many facts surging in the
client's mind that he will be unable to avoid a long recital of
them. The counselor can often perform some subtle redirection
in such cases by taking advantage of any further pauses in the
story and again responding to the feelings that have just been
expressed, and keeping the general pattern of facts at the back
of his mind for possible later attention when the client may
need some help to clarify his attitudes.

In this way, as the counselor responds acceptingly and with

genuine interest to the client's expressions of feeling, the client may gradually come to accept the "cue" that the counselor is interested in how he feels, and then he will feel free to go on to a progressively deeper unburdening of feelings. The interview will then come "alive," and counselor and client will achieve communication and rapport on a deeper and deeper level.

Some alternative kinds of responses on the part of the counselor may be illustrated by an actual example. Here, for her first interview, is Betty Brown, and in the course of an intense outpouring of indignation about Frank, her husband, goes on to say "The other evening when my mother was visiting me with my husband's knowledge and was invited to stay for the evening meal, Frank just didn't come home when he'd promised to do so, and when I got in touch with his office there was no answer. I felt deeply humiliated, and we just had to go on with the meal after giving him an hour's grace. Then at about ten o'clock he arrived with three of his objectionable friends, all of them the worse for alcohol, and they took possession of the lounge and went on with their rough party there, demanding that I bring them drinks from the refrigerator. I started to do that to keep the peace, but my mother started to tell Frank what she thought of him, and he savagely pushed her right into the sideboard, so that she got a bad cut in her head. And all Frank and his friends did was to laugh at her!" What kind of comment could the counselor make at this point?

a. "What happened then?" This would encourage Betty to rake up all the facts about Frank's conduct that she could think of, and the whole interview would be cluttered up with a mass of detail that would make the counselor's work almost impossible from the point of view of helping Betty to clarify her feelings and to achieve insight into the deeper aspects of the situation. A succession of facts would be appropriate in a legal action for divorce or for custody of the children or for maintenance, but not for the healing activity which is the aim and purpose of counseling.

b. "Frank had no right to do that!" However true this may be, it would not assist the counseling process at all to make such a comment. It would only add to Betty's resentment, and she would almost certainly throw the counselor's statement at Frank in their next conflict. When she tells Frank "The counselor said you had no right to do that!" one can well imagine how hopeless any attempt to gain Frank's confidence and cooperation in the counseling would be. The counselor is in no position to judge this issue, or indeed any issues, because he has no chance of assessing all the varied and complex factors which combine to induce any person to think and act in any particular way. He has not even any way of making sure that a client is telling "the truth, the whole truth, and nothing but the truth."

c. "You should have told him off properly and refused to have anything to do with the affair." Or "You should have realized he wasn't responsible for his actions at that time, and stopped your mother from interfering. She got what was coming to her!" Here again we have the entirely unwarranted judgment of the situation in two quite opposing ways, presumably dictated by the emotional prejudices of the "counselor," together with some quite superficial and prejudiced advice. No such attitude as this would do anything but harm to the whole counseling process. Betty will have had plenty of such advice from many quarters, to her increasing confusion, because either the different suggestions are irreconcilable, or she would feel them impracticable or futile. This kind of comment will only increase her resentment against Frank, or stir up some quite natural resentment against the counselor. Any chance of better insight and understanding would be ruined.

d. "Are you sure you haven't done anything to Frank to make him want to stay out and get drunk?" It may well be that Betty has had some part in the conflict and has been "needling" Frank in some way as to make him "fed up" with things, but this is certainly not the time or the way to approach that possibility. Betty in her indignation at Frank's conduct will be quite unable to see any part that she might have played in the conflict, and will resent the counselor's suggestion to the point of breaking the rapport, possibly beyond repair. She will not be at all likely to develop insight through such external suggestions until her pent up feelings are fully unburdened, and even then insight is much more likely to arise spontaneously from within than to be "injected" from without.

e. "You poor little girl, you shouldn't have to put up with such cruel treatment!" Here again such a statement may be quite true, but it will not be likely to help in the healing process for the counselor to identify himself with Betty in this way. It will tend to increase her self-pity and her indignation, as many other comments of this kind that she has received will have done. It is also likely that she will throw this comment at Frank next time there is an argument, "The counselor said that I shouldn't have to put up with such cruel treatment!" This will almost certainly ruin any chance of making good contact with Frank, and of being a healing influence in the marital situation.

f. "Don't worry about that, I've seen many cases much worse than that which do very well with counseling!" This also may be quite true, but such a comment is completely inappropriate in counseling. The counselor is in no position at this point to give any reassurance, and such a comment is much more likely for the purpose of relieving the counselor's anxiety than of helping the client. The client will know quite well that any such reassurance cannot be warranted at this stage, and will lose faith in the counselor's ability, and even his honesty and integrity, very quickly. Every counselor owes it to all his clients to be scrupulously honest in his comments and his attitudes.

g. "You felt pretty upset and humiliated about it?" Here is a simple accepting response to Betty's feelings, which will encourage her to go on unburdening them in a way that she will probably never have had a chance to do before this. To accept her feelings in this way does not mean that the counselor is judging the situation in any way. He is not saying that she ought to feel like that, or that Frank ought not to have done it, but simply that he realizes that she felt that way. The counselor has registered the facts in the back of his mind, but he has responded to the feelings, and in this way he is communicating to Betty that he is interested in the facts mainly for what they mean to her. He is inter-viewing, looking at her situation with her, feeling into her feelings without being involved in them. In that way he can provide a firm reliable support and can help to "lift" her spirit in a way that would be impossible if he were identified with her in her feelings as her own relatives might be.

This attitude of "feeling into" the client's feelings is generally called "empathy." The word comes from a German word "Einfühlung," which in its turn came from two Greek words which can be translated "In" and "Feeling." It differs from sympathy ("I feel as you do") and from antipathy ("I can't see why you should feel that way") and apathy ("I couldn't care less!"). It is trying to say something like "I'm beginning to realize how you feel." There is compassion in it, but also sufficient dispassion to prevent emotional identification which would deprive the counselor of the necessary objective perspective to help the client help himself.

Empathy in this sense would seem to be the counselor's most important contribution to the establishment and maintenance of healthy rapport, and it is therefore one of the foundations of counseling. It is an expression of the counselor's unconditional readiness to "feel into" the client, to look at his difficulties and problems, and his efforts to deal with them, through the client's eyes, and thus to provide him with a kind of new dimension in which he can come to consider his problems and their possible solutions. Above all, and whether there may be any adequate solution or not, the counselor provides the renewed encouragement of a healthy accepting personal relationship for the client's growth to greater maturity and understanding.

Empathy is not an easy quality to achieve or maintain. The counselor, being human, will have his share of emotions, prejudices, needs, and habitual attitudes, many of which may be evoked by the client's story and expressed feelings. It is all too easy for the counselor to respond in any of the ways already mentioned, fact-finding, moralizing, advising, criticizing, sympathizing, or reassuring respectively. Or he may plunge prematurely into the "practical" question, "What are you going to do about it?" To give genuine empathy any counselor needs to be aware of most of his own emotional needs and habitual attitudes and prejudices, so that he can allow for them, and be on guard against their intrusion into the counseling process. Even the most "accepting" words can be said in such a manner as to convey indifference, criticism, and even hostility, and the counselor needs constantly to ask himself the honest questions, "Am I being too protective to this person?" "Why did that remark stir up these feelings in me?" In this way, and by regular frank discussion of his work with other counselors, he may be helped to greater emotional steadiness, and the ability to offer genuine warmth without sentimentality.

To return to the counselor's response to Betty, "You felt pretty upset and humiliated about it?" This will give Betty the chance to confirm his impression of her feelings, or if she wishes to modify or extend it. It will certainly give her the feeling that here is someone ready to look honestly at her difficulty with her, and not to try to argue her out of her feelings or pat her condescendingly on the back. She will have the growing feeling that at least she can take the risk of being her real self. As this happens she will feel freer to talk about many things previously regarded as too threatening to her self-respect, and as she finds even these things accepted by the counselor, and herself accepted in spite of them, her defenses will go down and she will become, possibly for the first time, able to "come to herself," as the Prodigal did. Of course this may not all happen in the initial interview, but when the counselor handles the initial interview well the insight-generating process will become well established.

In many cases it is found that as the unburdening goes on the initial expression of mainly negative feelings, and reports about the partner's misdeeds will be gradually replaced by more positive expressions. At the beginning the positive expressions may be mixed up with the negative, love and hostility, independence and dependence, confidence and anxiety or doubt. This is called "ambivalence," and it is present to a considerable extent as "mixed feelings" in everyone. When it comes out in counseling the client may feel that there must be something abnormal in having such "contrary" feelings, and the counselor can best handle this situation by a simple accepting response to the ambivalent feelings.

For example, in the course of her further narrative Betty may say something like, "And yet with all those beastly things he's done I know he is good at heart and I still can't help loving him. There must be something peculiar about me!" The counselor's response might be something like, "Even though you can't bear a lot of his behavior you still feel he's lovable deep down?" The counselor's simple "matter of fact" acceptance of the ambivalence will generally do more to help the client than any vigorous assurance that "everybody has mixed feelings like that at times."

When the counselor makes the first response, "Even though you can't bear a lot of his behavior, you still feel he's lovable deep down?" it is quite likely that Betty will go on in some more positive expressions, such as "Yes, he's a good man at heart, I think he must have been going through a pretty worrisome time. If we could only get some of these horrible squabbles cleared up I'm sure we could be very happy, as we used to be." From being almost entirely dominated by her sense of humiliation and hostility, Betty has now come quite spontaneously, through the counseling relationship, to a much more objective and positive view of her situation, and a readiness to move ahead towards growth and healing of the marital relationship. She will go home from this interview much more relaxed and restrained, not approving Frank's crude and ill-mannered actions any more than she did, but ready to accept him and to see that he may be struggling with himself and not always able to cope adequately with his feelings.

Whatever may happen with any counseling with Frank, Betty will still have a lot more to do if she is to achieve sufficient understanding of her own vulnerabilities to work towards a lasting marital harmony, and Frank too will need to do the same. It takes two to make a partnership, but only one to destroy it. But even if Frank were unwilling to come it is possible to do something quite worthwhile through Betty if she can grow in maturity and learn to handle Frank's childish outbursts with dignity, with sustained acceptance of him coupled with a frankly expressed disapproval of his uncooperative behavior. Many marital disorders are very greatly healed by the ability of the more far-seeing partner to rise to the challenge with the help of a good counselor, and develop the mature capacity to accept other people and their feelings even though disapproving of their conduct. Here surely is the essence of personal relationship in society as well as in domestic life.

At some point in the interviewing, often towards the end of the initial interview but not necessarily so, it may be helpful for the counselor to make some attempt to define the goals and purposes of the counseling. In this way it may become clear to the client that he or she may through it be helped to greater understanding, greater growth to maturity, and greater ability to deal constructively with personal relationships. This may correct any assumption that the counselor will "do something" to bring peace and concord, or that he may "bring the partner to his senses" or "make him see that——." Then it is more likely that counselor and client will work toward the same end.

The client will often provide the opening for such definition of the aims of counseling by some question or remark. As the unburdening of the first or a later interview seems to be nearing its end a client will often ask some such question as "Now I've told you about the sorry affair, what you going to do about it?" This question may be implied rather than asked directly, but in either case it provides the counselor with the opportunity to deal with a misconception which may lead him and the client to work at cross purposes unless it is corrected.

The definition is generally best carried out tactfully, so as not to give any feeling of rejection. An example of the counselor's response might be, "You are hoping that I might be able to offer a solution to your problem? What kind of help were you hoping I might be able to give?" The client may either convey any underlying expectations regarding the counseling, or may throw it back to the counselor with some such remark as, "I really don't know, but I thought you'd have some ideas to suggest," or "I hoped you'd be able to do something to help."

The counselor might then respond in such a manner as, "I imagine you've already had quite a bit of advice, and been rather disappointed that it hasn't helped very much. Most of us find that in such complex things as the intimate personal relationships of marriage the best help we can give is to look with each person at his or her problems so that we can come to understand something of how they feel about it, and then to see if together we can come to understand better why they feel as they do. By talking the situation over as fully as possible in this way we find that people can come to see their situation and that of their partner more clearly. They are then better able to look at the various alternatives and decide what they can do about it without being confused by their upset feelings. I think you can see that this would be likely to need a few more sessions, and if you would like to go on I shall be glad to hear more of how you feel about it, and to look with you at anything you feel able to talk about." This might not be offered at such length in one "speech," but it represents the kind of definition that many clients may need in their unfamiliarity with the aims and methods of counseling.

A similar kind of definition may be given in response to another type of question by the client, "What do you think I should do about this?" The counselor's response might be, "What alternatives had you in mind? Perhaps we could look at them for a minute so that we could think about them between now and the next session." If they are given by the client, the counselor might then say, "Do you think it might be best to look more deeply into these so that we can find a really worthwhile answer to the problem?" Then he can go on to define the counseling aims as before.

At some point in this discussion it is generally important for the counselor to emphasize that everything discussed in every session of counseling is held in sacred confidence and not disclosed to anyone, even the marital partner, without the client's permission. There may be many kinds of natural openings for this, for example when the client expresses the feeling of some kind of disloyalty in discussing a marital partner or a parent or parent-in-law; or when the client seems diffident about discussing matters of immorality or possible mental illness. Such assurances will often overcome the client's reticence and greatly assist in the establishment of rapport.

3. TERMINATION OF THE INTERVIEW

As a general rule it is found that about fifty to sixty minutes is an appropriate time for any interview, unless there are special circumstances that make variation necessary. The client will generally be unable to profit sufficiently by any longer interview, and the counselor will generally have other responsibilities to discharge. There are some dependent types of client who seem to have a need to prolong interviews, and when the time is approaching for the termination they will bring up some new and important matter for discussion. Even at some expense to the rapport it is generally wise for any counselor to hold his clients tactfully but firmly to the realities of time; this is probably good for the client's education in "reality thinking." If the counselor allows the client to dictate the time of interviews there will come a time when the counselor is actually unable to spare extra time and this will cause great feeling of rejection to a client who has been allowed to be the "spoiled child" in this way previously.

It is generally important to leave the client with some more positive hopeful ideas at the end of any interview, and the counselor needs to prepare for this, beginning at about ten minutes before the termination. He tries to avoid matters which are heavily charged with feeling at that time, and he also tries to lead up to a simple summary of what has been expressed and what has been planned, if anything. The general introduction to this terminal stage of the interview may be something like this, "I'm afraid we're coming near the end of our time, and I can see that you still have some important things to work out. But perhaps we might try to summarize what we have managed to consider together and what may be worth thinking about before next time. Then we can have time at the next session to go more fully into what you may want to talk over." If necessary the counselor can bring up some encouraging thing that has come up in the interview, so as to conclude on as optimistic a note as possible, but it would not generally be helpful to drag in any optimistic assurance which has not been warranted.

The client should always feel quite free to decide whether or not to make another appointment, and if no appointment is made he should be assured that he can always come again if he should feel any desire to make another appointment.

4. THE INITIAL INTERVIEW WITH THE SECOND PARTNER

If the second partner doesn't come spontaneously it is generally wise for the counselor, with the first partner's permission, to write to him in some such terms as previously described. "Dear Mr.——, Your wife has been to see me for help in the marital situation that has arisen between you. I think I could be of more help if I could have the opportunity of hearing how you feel about it. If you can manage to come for a talk

I would be glad if you would make an appointment at a mutually suitable time. Yours faithfully, ———." To ask or allow the first partner to invite him may fail because he may say "no" on principle because of the conflict with his wife. To call him on the telephone would be asking him to make an immediate decision, which is not fair, and might block his acceptance. He can carry a letter around in his pocket for some days, and think it over carefully before deciding, and his decision is then more in line with his real feelings.

The actual initial interview with the second partner will often begin more cautiously than that with the first as we have seen but with adept sensitive handling the rapport will generally come quite quickly.

This interview might begin with a simple understanding kind of comment after the formal greeting, such as, "I'm glad you were able to come, I imagine you've had your share of worry in all this." In the case of Betty and Frank already mentioned, the interview with Frank might then open up in some such manner as this:

F. Yes, it hasn't been very pleasant, we seem to get more more and more in each other's hair, and I don't seem to be able to make the grade in Betty's expectations.

C. Would you like to tell me how you feel about the whole business; where you think the conflicts seem to be between you?

F. I suppose the main conflict comes because I constantly feel that Betty is trying to mold me into a kind of pattern that isn't me at all and couldn't be me. I'm supposed to be the good handyman and the good domestic help when required, and when I don't fit in with these quite rigid expectations there's a row. Not a momentary row either, it goes on sometimes for days, and if I ask her to stop picking at me she just gets more and more persistent with a kind of determination to wear me down. All I can do is to walk out and stay out for a time, I've even walked round the street for hours when there's nothing else I'd feel able to do. Betty little realizes what an effort it sometimes takes for me to come home, knowing that the strife is going to be on, and wondering whether I'll be able to control myself and avoid violence. I've managed it mostly so far, except for an unfortunate accident with her mother when she started to pick at me, but I can't feel sure that I'll always be able to restrain myself.

c. You feel pretty fed up with the pressure on your personality, and you can't get Betty to realize that?

F. If she only knew, that sort of thing only makes me all the more determined to hang on to the little bit of freedom I seem to be able to preserve. There are even times when I can't resist the urge to do things that upset her just to prove to myself as well as to her that I'm not going to be molded to her pattern. And that only seems to make her even more determined to organize me. Now she's getting more and more distant and even sulking at times, as if I'm a sort of intruder in the house. When I try to make any loving approach as likely as not she'll just push me away as if she hated the ground I walked on. And yet I know that's not really how she feels, she used to be the most demonstrative soul. I've thought about it from every possible angle, and I can only think she's going through a lot of strife inside herself. I know I've handled things pretty badly at times and at other times I've been so troubled that I've forgotten things I should have remembered. Do you think there's any chance that things between us can be straightened out, I've got pretty despairing about the whole business.

c. It looks to you as if Betty is struggling a bit too, and you're both ready to make a real effort to find a better understanding. Do you feel that there must be some real hope that two sensible adults who both want to do so will be able, with a bit of help, to find the way to better understanding and cooperation?

F. Yes, I feel much more hopeful than I did, I think this has only just come in time. I'm ready to give it all I've got, and if we can't work out something this time I'm afraid it's all up.

c. This is it. You're ready to get right down into the whole thing?

F. Yes, it looks as if we've got to go deeper than we've so far been able to do if we're to get anywhere, and I think we're both ready for a shot at that. If we could know why we react to each other in such stupid ways, and stir up more conflict when we want to improve the feeling between us, I think it would help tremendously. But it seems a bit too difficult so far. I don't feel very expert at what you call "getting right down into the whole thing," and I'll probably need some help in understanding the kind of thing you want. But I feel better for this discussion, I'm even beginning to feel interested in how this sort of thing works. I'm afraid I was a bit vague about what I was letting myself in for. After Betty had had an open go with you, and probably told you some hair raising things about me, I wondered what you'd think about me.

c. You'd thought I might do a bit of judging?

F. Well . . . yes, that's what everybody else she's talked to seems to have done, without much interest into any of my feelings about the sorry business. I've kept things pretty much to myself, I haven't felt that it would do any good to go talking and telling tales on

Betty to anyone, even to my mother. It seems a bit dis-
loyal to me. I didn't even intend to tell you much about
her, but somehow it came out and I'm glad I've been
able to let off some steam. I suppose I'll have to look
at some of my own less pleasant qualities too, and I
think I can make a genuine attempt to do that.

It looks as if Frank is taking a little time to get down to the
job and taking some temporary refuge in generalities, possibly
helped to this by the counselor's response to his question about
whether there's any chance that things can be straightened
out. But the counselor has let him take his time to come round,
and the rapport seems good at this point.

What has been described so far is obviously a brief summary of the main threads in the initial interview with Betty
and the first part of the initial interview with Frank. Many
of the invariable deviations from the main threads have been
left out for purposes of clarity and length. But this account
may illustrate something of the kind of attitude and method
of handling the initial interviews in the attempt to achieve
good rapport with each partner, and to prepare the way for
some deeper exploration with them. It also illustrates some
natural feelings of the second partner in coming for counseling and the relief that comes from the counselor's acceptance
of them, which may open the way, as with Frank, for the
greater unburdening of feeling than he had previously felt
able to do. The acceptance of these feelings helps to lay the
foundation for a healthy rapport. Without this rapport, it might
well be impossible for many men to risk baring their souls concerning matters about which they feel rather uncomfortable
and even ashamed, but which have to be worked through if
partners are to be freed for spontaneous relationships with each
other.

5. SOME SIGNIFICANT MENTAL PROCESSES
FOUND IN COUNSELING

Before leaving the subject of the initial interviewing of the two partners we may consider some important mental processes which may occur in either client and some which may occur in the counselor during the first or any subsequent interviews. How these are handled will make a profound difference to the success or failure of the counseling, and they are therefore worthy of consideration at this stage.

In the client some of the more common mental processes are the emotional unburdening which is called catharsis and the expression of "contrary" feelings described as ambivalence, which have already been dealt with to some extent. Other common mental processes in the client are repression, rationalization, suppression, compensation, abreaction, anxiety, resistance and "blocking," projection, transference, insight formation, redefinition and "reconceptualization," and sublimation. In the counselor many of these processes may be evoked by the emotional interaction of counseling, and two others, "counter-transference" and identification are worthy of some attention.

a. *Repression.* It is clear that unless people's consciousness were freed from the infinite number and variety of memories of unimportant things, any intelligent living would be impossible. This process of automatic "forgetting" is called repression, and it is essential to realize that it is an unconscious and not a deliberate process. As many obsessed people find to their dismay the harder they try to push any thought out of their minds the more it will keep on intruding. Repression therefore is a universal and healthy process in this sense. But it can also be unhealthy in that some of our most painful and distressing unresolved experiences are automatically "forgotten," and when that happens the emotional tensions associated with them are apt to go on "festering" below the level of awareness and to produce all kinds of apparently irrational feelings and ideas, and even disturbances of bodily function. Many previous attitudes and actions of which we feel ashamed are automatically repressed in this way from our awareness, but they may be clearly remembered by those with whom we live.

One result of this is that often in counseling one partner may admit no recollection of some aggressive act of which the other one complains bitterly, and he is accused of deliberate lying. It helps greatly if the counselor realizes that in fact the incident may have been genuinely "forgotten," particularly if it originally occurred in a quarrel that was highly charged with emotion. Some clarification of this with the aggrieved partner may help to reduce the tension.

Some of the mental processes about to be discussed are results of repression or reactions to it, and these aspects of repression will be dealt with when these processes are considered.

It is not the counselor's function to attempt to bring deeply repressed material to the "surface." That is for the trained psychotherapist to carry out in individual psychotherapy. But many of the client's partly repressed experiences in the recent or more distant past may come into memory as the counseling proceeds, and may emerge in the emotional unburdening. The counselor accepts the feelings expressed in the setting of his attention to the relationship, and does not set out on any attempt at deep dynamic interpretations, for which of course he is not equipped. But without some attention to the underlying, at least partially repressed elements in the situation, marriage counseling, and counseling in general, would fail to meet most of the disorders for which it is sought.

b. *Rationalization.* Like repression, this is a universal mental process, one of the automatic "protective" devices for human self-regard. It is an outcome of repression in that the real motives for many of our feelings, attitudes and actions are conveniently "blotted out," and we bluff ourselves into the plausible belief in a more "respectable" reason for what we have felt and done. This is often quite unconvincing to many other people, who may "see through" our apparent hypocrisies and shams, and may make no secret of their doing so, even though they will almost certainly be rationalizing many similar things in their own lives.

When such accusations are made or implied all our defenses become mobilized and we tend to react emotionally, which brings further emotional reactions in the accusers, and the battle is on. It seems that most people tend to criticize in others the very things to which the critics are unconsciously prone. "The pot calls the kettle black," well could the poet Robert Burns observe hauntingly, in his poem, "To a Louse":

> O wad some Pow'r the giftie gie us
> To see oursels as others see us!
> It wad frae mony a blunder free us,
>   And foolish notion.

In marriage counseling every narrative of each client tends to be filled with rationalizations, and most of the necessary insight is concerned with the ability to "see through" some of one's own rationalizations. Since any attempt at "frontal attack" on most rationalization will only tend to stir up more defenses, the counselor restrains himself from any such temptation and accepts the client's expressed feelings in the manner already described. As the counseling sessions proceed he will help the client to "clarify" his feelings and attitudes, and possibly those of his partner. This will be discussed in the section dealing with the subsequent interviews.

c. *Suppression.* This term is used to describe the deliberate withholding of possibly significant elements in the marital conflict from discussion, generally as an attempt to preserve self-regard. In this way it is differentiated from repression which is an automatic unconscious process. Suppression is to some extent inevitable and quite natural in counseling, because the client generally will feel the need to "try out" the counselor before he can risk the disclosure of anything which might incur the risk of rejection or condemnation. This again has much to do with repressed fears of childhood parent figures by whom the client may have felt rejected at a "helpless" time when such rejection was a "life and death" matter.

The counselor, realizing this, will always keep the situation open and allow for many deeper elements to emerge in their own time as the client "tests him out" by guarded tentative admissions, progressively gaining confidence through the counselor's acceptance of all of them. It is often found that these previously suppressed elements prove to be the most important keys to better insight and better relationships. In some cases important suppressed material can be brought into the open more quickly through a joint interview when certain safeguards have been established. This will be discussed in more detail in the section which deals with the arranging and handling of joint interviews.

d. *Compensation.* As it applies to the mental processes found in counseling compensation is an unconscious mental process by which the discomfort and humiliation of some defect in character, ability or behavior are relieved by the over-emphasis on an opposite quality of personality. Self assertiveness, for example, is often an unconscious automatic compensation for deep and puzzling feelings of inferiority, which in their turn may be the products of repressed humiliating experiences. Many such compensations are of healthy positive value, as Adler has repeatedly emphasized in his psychological writings. But many others are productive of strain and conflict in the individual and in his personal relationships, and these may have great significance in the counseling process.

For example a husband who seems bent on taking every possible opportunity to humiliate his wife in all kinds of unjust and even irrational ways will generally be found to be suffering from a deep sense of inferiority, failure or guilt, but this may take much time and patience in counseling for it to become clear to this husband. But when the counselor sees the signs of it he is more ready to keep the door open to the client's gradual achievement of insight.

One suggestive indication by which over-compensation can be suspected is a kind of compulsive quality in the attitudes and behavior of the client, as if he were possessed by the particular need. This is found most typically in the neurotic personality, but it is also found to a variable extent in many immature people and in others who show no other evidence of neurotic traits. As long as the counselor keeps in his mind the possibility of compensatory attitudes he is less likely to be bluffed into taking his clients' feelings and attitudes and their behavior at their face value. At the appropriate point a deeply understanding comment, "Could it be that your need to humiliate your wife comes from a deep sense of failure in yourself?" might bring a flash of insight to the client. But of course such comments will only be appropriate when the counseling has gone beyond the initial stages of catharsis and the development of rapport.

e. *Abreaction.* This is a process, more commonly found in psychotherapy than in counseling, in which the unburdening of emotion gathers such "momentum" that the client is completely possessed by it for a time. His speech may be quite unrestrained in content and in emphasis, and the outpouring of emotion may be accompanied by all kinds of bodily movements and expressions. In some cases of psychotherapy this kind of release of feeling is encouraged by free association, by hypnosis or by certain sedative drugs, but this requires considerable professional training and experience if it is to be handled without the risk of harm.

In counseling abreaction is not generally encouraged, and when it begins to appear the counselor needs to consider carefully whether to allow it to proceed or whether to offer the client the opportunity to defer the interview. When abreaction appears in a joint interview it is particularly important to consider the risk of unduly wounding the other partner, and to be ready to terminate this part of the interview if this appears to be possible. The abreacting partner may be given the opportunity to unburden his intense feelings to the counselor when the other partner has been allowed to withdraw for the time, and that may be of considerable help to the "inflamed" client.

f. *Anxiety.* We are here concerned with anxiety as it may develop in the counseling process, and it may do so in the counselor or the client, or in both. Many clients feel some anxiety at the idea of coming for help, and this anxiety should gradually diminish as they come to feel the counselor's acceptance. The kind of anxiety which the client may develop in the actual counseling is something every counselor needs to be ready to perceive and to deal with. This is most likely to occur when the client suddenly comes to feel that his emotions are taking hold of him and that he is getting "out of his depth." He may show this anxiety either in facial expression, bodily restlessness, inflection of speech, or by suddenly withdrawing into his shell. Sometimes he may even terminate the counseling abruptly. It is essential for the counselor to try to perceive this before it becomes too intense, and to avoid any "pushing" in his attitude or in his comments. When the anxiety seems to be increasing it is often well to offer the client a rest from the counseling. If he wishes to go on he is allowed to do so, but in many cases an anxious client accepts the offer of a rest quite eagerly, and can then return more easily to the anxiety producing material in a later session.

Anxiety may arise in the counselor when a client seems to be uncooperative or resistant to the counseling, especially when the client indulges in prolonged silences. The anxious counselor is then tempted to resort to a succession of questions rather than to show complete acceptance of the client's possible feelings, and that will tend to delay or divert the counseling and may even spoil it altogether.

g. *Resistance and "blocking."* These processes may commonly occur in counseling and need to be understood by the counselor. In some cases the "blocking" may be due to the unconscious identification of the counselor with someone in the client's early or present life, of whom the client has been frightened, or felt hatred, distrust, or some other negative emotion. In other cases it may be due to growing anxiety in the client, and it is then a very useful automatic "delaying mechanism" which secures for the client some time to become adapted to the new situation.

If the counselor jumps to the conclusion that resistance is a deliberate act of the client he may well become hostile or anxious. These feelings will inevitably be communicated to the client, however much the counselor may think he has hidden them, and the client's anxiety or hostility will be increased. When the counselor understands that these processes are generally automatic and necessary he will find it easier to accept them and to show his acceptance, and then the client will be better able to work through them. In some cases in which a prolonged "blocking" seems to be due to the client's identification of the counselor with a significant figure in his background it may be most helpful for the counselor to refer the client to another counselor, possibly one of the opposite sex or one in a different age group. In many cases this has freed the client from the blocking and enabled him to work through the earlier relationship to a healthy acceptance. In some cases of such identification it may be found that the same negative feelings were projected onto the marital partner, and then the working through them will greatly help the marital relationship as well as the actual counseling process. Resistance and blocking therefore are important processes for the counselor to accept and to use constructively in the later clarification.

h. *Projection.* This is another of the reactions to repressed ideas and feelings, in which painful or unpleasant ideas and feelings are rejected from awareness automatically, but the discomfort arising from their inner "festering" seeks relief by irrational displacement onto some other person or external agency. As previously noted in the discussion of repression we tend to criticize in others the very faults to which we are most prone and most averse to recognizing. In many cases this is an automatic unconscious mental device, and our criticisms do not appear irrational to us. When the victim of our accusations reacts to what he feels a rank and unwarranted injustice we accuse him of hypocrisy or dishonesty and the emotional conflict is away to a vigorous beginning.

Many of our projections are harmless enough, even if not at all helpful to our growth in realistic thinking. We ascribe our failures to such agencies as "bad luck" or "kismet" or to some other invulnerable agency, or to such influences as "the Government," "The Opposition Party," "The Church" or to some "Board" or other, which are large and invulnerable enough not to worry about it. But our projections may be more serious for ourselves when we blame "the job" or "the neighborhood" for something we are unable to recognize in ourselves and begin to act on such an irrational assumption by changing the external situation. Then the inner and unfaced difficulty still continues to haunt our minds, and we look for another "scapegoat," and perhaps go from job to job looking for what cannot be found in that way. Well could Shakespeare observe in "Julius Caesar," "The fault . . . is not in our stars, but in ourselves, that we are underlings."

In marriage counseling many of the accusations made by either partner toward the other are of this nature, and they may arise from many sources. Apart from the unjust accusation about something of which the accuser is really guilty there may be projections of hatred or other destructive emotion from earlier unsolved relationships with a parent or other significant figure. A wife whose childhood was continually harassed by a drunken father may easily react with bitter accusations when her husband has taken a very moderate and harmless amount of alcohol, and the husband's indignant response to this "injustice" will make things worse. A husband who has had an irritating and frustrating day at the office, and has been unable to express his feelings about it there for fear of losing his job, may come home and be bitterly cruel to his children who have done nothing to deserve any condemnation. The range and variety of manifestations of projection is infinite.

In some cases the mechanism of projection may have still more serious effects. When the repressed material is particularly painful and persistent, and sometimes when it is only partially repressed, it may appear in a person's consciousness as a complete distortion of reality, as a delusion or an hallucination. It is important for the counselor to recognize this possibility, but it is not his function to attempt to treat such conditions. Such cases where there is any possibility of this kind of distortion are appropriately referred to a psychiatrist, if possible through the person's own doctor. The counselor may have an important function in helping the other partner to cope with the difficult and most distressing situation, by recognition that the irrational partner cannot help being so, and by refraining from fruitless argument about the distortions while standing quietly firm on his own autonomy.

i. *Transference.* This is a particular kind of projection in which any client might re-enact toward the counselor any kind of intense feeling which was, or is, really directed, but insufficiently expressed, toward someone else, such as a parent or sibling, the marital partner, or some other significant figure. For example the client who as a child was continually humiliated, taunted or teased by a parent or sibling, or possibly by a sadistic school teacher, may accuse the counselor quite seriously of humiliating him, in some such manner as, "You just sit there like God Almighty, nodding as if you knew everything. I hoped for a bit of help, not humiliation!" When the client's parents were indifferent and cold to him as a child, and failed to talk to him, the counselor's silence, designed to allow him a good hearing, may be misinterpreted as indifference and aloofness, and the client will show the same kind of hostility as originally felt (but not able to be expressed) toward the parents.

If the counselor reacts to such feelings and accusations as if they were unwarranted attacks on himself it will only deepen the client's hostility and will probably ruin the counseling. This kind of emotional reaction to the client's transference is called "counter-transference," and it will be dealt with in a later part of this section.

It is the counselor's task to understand why such feelings may arise in the client, and to accept them so that the client will have the opportunity to work through them to a positive relationship with his own feelings and with his marital partner and other people. In psychotherapy the handling of transference is one of the most important aspects of the whole treatment, and transference is almost inevitable as the therapist makes contact with the surging dynamics of the patient's inner personality. Transference is less marked in the more superficial work of counseling, but with the intense emotional conflicts in marital disorders the counselor cannot avoid having to deal with some amount of transference.

Apart from the hostility already touched on there are other kinds of transference. A client may find in a counselor of the opposite sex an embodiment of the qualities looked for and not sufficiently found in the marriage, such as acceptance and interest, and may "fall in love" with the counselor. Even a counselor of the same sex as the client may quite unwittingly stir up some latent or actual homosexual feelings in the client with the same result. Almost any emotion, hostility and aggressiveness, romantic love, anxiety, cold indifference, and even deep morbid guilt, may be "transferred" onto the counselor without his deserving it in any way.

In most cases he can best show his acceptance of the transference by the kind of accepting "questioning" comment that has already been illustrated in earlier parts of this book, such as, "You feel very disappointed in what I've been able to do?" or "You're feeling pretty sore at me?" An important exception to this is where the client shows any indication of "falling in love" with the counselor. If the counselor made such a comment as "You're feeling in love with me?" it would almost certainly cause extreme anxiety in the client and upset the counseling beyond repair. The counselor's best approach is probably a simple non-verbal acceptance of the feeling, unless it is verbally expressed directly by the client, and careful avoidance of any word or action that would possibly add to the client's feeling.

One of the greatest services any counselor or psychotherapist can offer to any troubled person is to allow the person the opportunity progressively to express the less "respectable" aspects of his personality and to find that he is accepted in spite of them. Many such people have never felt really accepted "for themselves alone." They have come to the deeply set conviction that they can never live up to what would be necessary for other people's acceptance, without which they cannot accept themselves. The counselor's simple acceptance of any such client, progressively tested and tried by more and more expression of aspects of his personality of which he is ashamed or apprehensive, will gradually release the client from many of these inner hindrances to naturalness and self-acceptance. Then there is no need for many of his automatic defensive reactions which had stirred up so much conflict with his marital partner, his "boss," his children or others.

In doing this the counselor cannot avoid overlapping into the field of psychotherapy, but if he keeps the relationship between the partners as the central focus of his work he will not generally go far beyond his depth. The fact that he has good rapport with the client will often give him more chance for good therapy in such situations than the therapist would have in the absence of established rapport at this stage. But if the difficulty shows itself as mainly in the inner personality of any client the counselor should immediately consider the advisability of referral to a psychiatrist.

j. *Insight formation.* The most important aspect of this mental process for the counselor to appreciate is that it is something that is achieved by the client, and not something that is communicated to him by the counselor or anyone else. Most people have a rather naive faith in the power of the spoken word, naive in the sense that it is extended to apply to people in emotional conflict and tension. In marital situations which come to the counselor the partners almost invariably have been the recipients of many wise observations, so obviously rational and appropriate to those who have offered them, but almost completely ineffective in the marital conflict. Such wise and well-meant homilies do not touch the deep unconscious elements in the situation, and however much the partners attempt to follow them, their efforts are superficial in this sense and have to be sustained continually by "will power" which inevitably breaks down after a time and in the face of unexpected provocations.

Intellectual insight in this sense does not necessarily involve a person's emotional attitudes, and in such cases will not have any deep or sustained influence on behavior. But when through patient working through intense and conflicting feelings in the accepting, non-threatening atmosphere of good counseling, a person comes to awareness of his emotional needs and their effects on his previous attitudes, he is then able and ready to change from within. What we discover for ourselves is always more influential than what is communicated to us from without.

Insight formation then is something achieved by clients and it involves all aspects of the personality. The counselor's task is mainly to facilitate the process by acceptance and by "reflecting" the client's feelings and looking with him at their implications. It is to be a kind of psychic "mirror" in which the client can come gradually to see into his own personality and into the significant elements in the disturbed relationships, so as to be able to make whatever changes he may feel disposed to do.

k. *Redefinition and "re-conceptualization."* These closely related processes are really part of the process of insight, or at least an application of insight to the many different aspects of the client's personal attitudes and relationships. As new insights dawn the client will often begin enthusiastically to rethink these things with new interest and hope. This process will generally go on as much or more between the counseling sessions as within them, and it will often continue after the conclusion of counseling. The counselor may be asked to look with the client at many of his tentative conclusions, and to help in further clarification with either or both clients. Sometimes after an interval of some months after the conclusion of the main series of interviews some further matters may come up for clarification in an extra session, and the discussion is then likely to be on a very positive practical level and to result in further consolidation of the partnership.

1. *Sublimation.* When feelings of any kind are strong it may be harmful to the personality to try to suppress or block them. The mechanism of sublimation is one through which many such potentially destructive feelings can be re-channeled into socially acceptable attitudes. For example hostility is often strongly imbedded in the human personality, and men and women will always tend to feel angry under certain conditions. But this anger can be diverted into the socially acceptable channel of a vigorous campaign against the common enemies of mankind rather than allowed to cause useless and destructive family squabbles. The ability to sublimate feelings varies greatly with different people; it is almost absent, for example, in the psychopathic personality and strongly present in the saint. It can be developed by spiritual inspiration and discipline and helped by such activities as healthy cooperative sport and good hobbies in which enthusiasms can be shared. It can also be helped by education when the personal relationship with the educators is good. The marriage counselor may help firstly by his knowledge of the value of this mechanism, and secondly by his personal inspiration of the client and his willingness to go along with him as he works through the slow healing process.

Some other mental mechanisms, such as phantasy thinking and symbolic thinking, fixation and regression, may be found in the counseling of some people, but they are more appropriate to psychotherapy than to counseling and will therefore not be dealt with in any detail. If they show up to any extent in marriage counseling the counselor may well consider the advisability of referral to a psychotherapist.

There are two important mental mechanisms which may often occur in the counselor apart from those already dealt with in connection with their occurrence in the client. These are "counter-transference" and "identification."

m. *Counter-transference*. In common with all people the counsellor will inevitably have his share of habitual attitudes, prejudices and emotional needs. It is important for counseling that he should be as aware of them as much as possible, so to minimize the risk of their intrusion into the counseling relationship to its great detriment. Some of this awareness should come during the selection interviews and during the counselor's training and his "in-service" training. But with human fallibility as it is there is always the possibility of emotional needs in counselors beyond their own awareness, which may be "resurrected" by the emotional interaction of counseling.

For example a counselor may have a deep emotional need to be loved and admired, and be unaware of its real strength in him. Supposing now that in the course of counseling the client begins to show love and admiration to him, touching this deep and largely unrecognized emotional need. The counselor will then feel a deep inner pleasure in the relationship, and if he is not careful he might respond affectionately to the client's transference. This may lead to unhealthy emotional involvement which is bad for counselor and client, and even more destructive to the client's marital relationship.

If, on the other hand, a client shows intense hostility to a counselor who has a deep need to be loved and admired, it may well stir up great hostility in the counselor against the client, which will be communicated to him even when the counselor thinks he is hiding his hostile feelings. The situation is complicated further in marriage counseling because such hostility to one client may easily lead to some identification with the other one, the results of this on the marriage counseling need no emphasis.

It is necessary for any counselor to try to define his own attitude to clients in this regard. Is it necessary for him to show no love to any client? The situation might be clarified by suggesting that the love that is appropriate for a counselor to show is the "parental" kind of love rather than the "lover" kind of love. At its best the parental kind of love (without the deep emotional attachment of the parent-child relationship) is a genuine goodwill "without strings," a loving acceptance of the "child" for his own sake, a caring for his ultimate welfare without demanding any kind of return. This is what is meant by the Greek word "agapé" and represents Christian goodwill and any other goodwill of similar nature to it. This "parental" kind of love has sufficient dispassion in it to prevent the natural compassion from becoming too involved emotionally in the client—to prevent "empathy" from drifting into "sympathy."

With this kind of accepting goodwill the counselor, whatever his own emotional need to be loved, can accept love or hostility from a client without allowing himself to use the counseling relationship for his own benefit or gratification. He can keep the counseling relationship as one that is between two people for the benefit of one—the client!

Apart from a possible need to be loved and admired, a counselor can have many other emotional needs, the need to be agreed with or understood, the need to assert himself, the need to manipulate other people and their lives, and even the need to prove to himself by suffering what a "devoted" person he is. How can these needs be perceived by the counselor if they have not been brought to light in his training? Firstly, by regular opportunities for the receiving of counseling of some kind himself. This may come through case discussions with supervisors or senior counselors or consultants, or through deliberate approach to someone of this kind for counseling. Any counselor who finds his own emotions becoming stirred up unduly in his counseling should consider seeking help in whatever way he can, so that he can "sort out" his own unresolved conflicts and his emotional vulnerabilities and needs.

In addition to this, and when adequate help is not available, he may assist in his own "sorting out" by asking himself some crucial personal questions. Here are some typical questions which may come up in the counselor's mind about countertransference or identification:

Why did I feel strained or hostile to that person? What did he do or say to stir up my feelings like this? Am I vulnerable there?

Why was I so keen to get my ideas across to that person? Do I want people to think that I know all the answers about marriage?

Why was I so protective with that client who felt so unloved and rejected? Could it be that I feel a bit that way too?

Why was I so averse to the idea of writing to the husband of this client? Have I felt so identified with her that I am rejecting him without wanting to get any idea of how he feels?

Why did I get so defensive when the client misjudged my attitude? Do I expect that people should always understand me?

Why did I keep on asking questions in that way? Is it because I am really curious about people's intimate doings, or am

I being anxious to avoid long silences and risk the client thinking I'm not adept at counseling?

Any intense emotional reaction that arises in the counselor's mind in counseling should be at least the subject of some honest discussion with another counselor or a consultant. In this way the counselor can go on indefinitely with his own growth and improvement in counseling. It is highly probable that there are no counselors who are so competent that they cannot go on developing and learning.

A question that may come up many times in the counselor's mind when things do not seem to go as he had hoped is "Do I assume that I ought to be able to help everybody who comes to me? Can I accept my share of failure and try to learn from each one? Can I discuss my failures as well as my "successes" with my colleagues?

Of course it would be an impossibility for a counselor with any normal feelings to be completely unmoved by the tensions and sufferings of those who come for help. To keep one's emotions "on ice" as has sometimes been suggested, would mean that the client would feel no warmth of empathy, and might even feel completely rejected by an apparently indifferent counselor. The counselor's emotions need to be recognized and controlled rather than "frozen." When they are in any danger of taking control of the situation the counselor needs to face the situation and either regain control or consider referring the client to another counselor.

If a counselor finds himself or herself feeling particularly happy at the prospect of a forthcoming session with a particular client this is also an indication for some careful honest self-evaluation. Such feelings can easily grow to the point at which they may endanger the counseling and when not dealt with they may gradually corrode the counselor's personality and make for very faulty work. By its very nature counseling is difficult to supervise very closely, and the counselor can "get away" with many inappropriate inner feelings for a longer time than is healthy. Counselors are in positions of great trust and are under a solemn obligation to preserve an impeccable integrity in their inner attitudes as well as in their actual work.

n. *Identification.* It is very common for a counselor to be tempted to identify with a client whose feelings touch a sympathetic chord. This differs from counter-transference in that the counselor is responding to something experienced by a client rather than something experienced by himself directly from the client.

For example a female married counselor who has children of her own may be given a pathetic story by a female client of the husband's sadistic and sustained cruelty to their children. It may be that the counselor suffered from some such cruelty in her own childhood, and has been trying to give her own children a much better life than she received. Now the account of cruelty to the client's children, and the client's distress may well stir up very strong hostile feelings against the client's husband before she even sees him, coupled with considerable emotional identification with the client. She may either feel averse to seeing the husband at all, or if she does see him she may have a strong desire to let him know what she thinks of him.

If such feelings are strong it might be wise for her to arrange for another counselor to see the husband, and if necessary the wife too, because strong identification with the client will only add to her hostility against her husband, while the counselor's hostility would most likely spoil any chance of building rapport with the husband.

It is of course natural for such feelings to arise in the counselor under such conditions, but an important part of the inner resources of the counselor's personality is that she should be able to withhold judgment, and assume that there will be some set of reasons for the husband's cruelty. If she can control her feelings in some such manner as this and give full acceptance to the husband she may gain some idea of his feelings and his background, the uncritical assumptions and emotional needs behind his attitudes. Then, possibly in a joint session, the whole background conflict which contributed to the cruelty might come out in the only kind of atmosphere in which it could be constructively faced and dealt with.

Behind all such emotional reactions in any counselor there is a fundamental reality which sometimes needs to be recalled. We often allow ourselves to live in the unreal assumption that life should be always pleasant, and ignore the grim fact that suffering is a universal experience, an integral part of life as it has always been and as it will be as long as there is evil abroad in the world. Everyone who comes into any "helping" activity will come at some time to the realization so eloquently expressed by St. Paul, "We are not contending against flesh and blood, but against the principalities, against the powers, against the world rulers of this present darkness, against the spiritual hosts of wickedness in the heavenly places." (Ephesians, 6:12, R.S.V.) However they may regard it counselors need what St. Paul described as "the whole armor of God," the ability and strength to fight constructively against all unnecessary suffering, but to do so in such a manner as is most likely to overcome it "from the ground up," by inner healing of the disturbed personalities who in their bewilderment or despair would go on inflicting it. Contact with human suffering drives anyone with any regard for human beings back onto their own philosophy or their own religion, and constitutes a searching test of its adequacy and a challenge to continued growth and personal development.

Identification can occur in many other ways than that which has been discussed, and it is inevitable that a counselor will find things in the unburdening of his clients which resonate with his own inner feelings and his earlier and more recent experiences. But counselors are trained, and gain considerable practice in the art of keeping themselves out of the picture, and concentrating in genuine caring fashion on the welfare of the client in the long term more than the short term view.

This involves some real self-acceptance on the part of the counselor, without which it is very difficult to accept anyone else in any genuine fashion. There is always room for improvement in every counselor's inner resources of psychic strength and stamina, and counseling itself provides a very good opportunity for such improvement to happen as long as the counselor is honest with himself and open to a genuine search for help when he feels any need for it.

CHAPTER VI

The Subsequent Interviews
with Either Client

IN SUBSEQUENT INTERVIEWS with either client some deeper problems may be expressed, which for various reasons were not brought up earlier. The counselor needs always to have this possibility in mind and to keep an open mind for them. He may also help if he is sensitive to any rather cautious tentative approaches to such deeper matters, and able to respond in such a way as to encourage their full unburdening. One kind of tentative approach may be through an apparently general question, and if the counselor is induced to give a straight answer to it he might unwittingly "close the bidding" and discourage the client from going on. A constant unexpressed question at the back of the counselor's mind, "I wonder why she is asking that question" may help him to respond to the implied feeling, and "keep the bidding open."

For example in the interviews with Betty she changed the subject at one point by asking, apropos of nothing in particular, "Do you think husbands and wives ought to try always to please each other?" If the counselor gave the obvious answer, "Of course they should," with or without a pleasant little homily, it would probably close that part of the discussion and Betty would switch off on to another subject, or make some inconsequential observation. But supposing the counselor has his wits about him to the extent that he realizes that Betty would already know the answer to such a straight question, and must therefore have some interesting reason for asking it. Then he might respond in some such manner as, "You sometimes find it difficult to please Frank?" This would give Betty the chance to go into more detail, "Yes, I'm afraid I do in some ways," and this might well lead on to a full discussion of the sexual relationship and the despair Betty is feeling about meeting Frank's needs when he is not seeing any need to win her, but rather takes her compliance in sex intercourse for granted. It is obviously essential that this deeper area of their conflict needs to be explored, if possible with each of them, if a lasting solution to their conflicts is to be achieved.

We have seen that while the "unburdening" of either partner is proceeding the counselor is encouraging the progressive expression of feelings by responding to their expressed feelings rather than to the facts related in the narratives. But he is not discarding the facts, he is keeping them at the back of his mind for a very important purpose. He assesses the facts mainly in terms of what meaning they have for the client, how the client feels about them, and he more or less instinctively relates such reactions to what might be regarded as reasonable. As the story goes on he will begin to perceive a kind of pattern of reaction, through which he can gain increasing information about the personality of the client. This information may be considered from certain particular points of view for each client.

1. THE CLIENT'S "ROLE PERCEPTIONS" AND "ROLE EXPECTATIONS" IN MARRIAGE

Betty, for example may have expressed some feelings which suggest that she sees her "wifely" role as that of a domestic dictator, strictly administering the whole of the domestic organization with rigid efficiency, as Mary did in the first case described in this book. She may also have conveyed her "role expectatons" regarding husbands, that Frank should be a very efficient and enthusiastic "handyman," in which view she pestered him continually to do what he had never had any talent or enthusiasm for doing and preferred to pay a trades-man to do. Frank, on the other hand, may have expressed feel-ings which suggest that he sees the husband's role in marriage as in a very real sense "the head of the house" who must never descend to any kind of "domestic activity," such as drying the dishes or helping with looking after the children.

If the counselor is on the lookout for the nature of these role perceptions and expectations, then, when the main un-burdening of feeling has been completed, he may help the clients to clarify their attitudes by such a questioning com-ment as (to Betty), "You feel that Frank ought to fit in com-pletely with what you decide in running the home?" or "You look on the minor repairs as Frank's job?" With Frank, a possible comment may be something like, "You feel the hus-band should have no responsibility for helping in the domestic duties?" Frank and Betty are then able to respond either affirmatively, "Yes, that's how I feel about it," or to correct the counselor's comment, "Well, not quite to that extent, but I do think—."

In this way the role perceptions and expectations of each partner are brought to light and made quite definite, and the "role frustrations" also become clear. Later when there is a joint interview, it may be possible to put the feelings of each of them about roles in marriage alongside one another for comparison in a manner which would previously have been impossible for them to have managed on their own owing to the "intrusion" of intense emotional reactions. This clarification of role perceptions may enable them to come to some measure of mutual compromise at this level, which may be satisfactory to them when their troubles are not very deep or involved. Frank may feel "If that's all that's holding us up I could easily give Betty a bit more help in the domestic jobs." And Betty might say, "If Frank feels the organization so much I think I could relax a bit in the interests of peace and harmony."

The chief risk of such an agreement is that it may leave some very powerful underground influences untouched, and these may well be stirred up by some unintentional "hurt" or "neglect," and the subsequent disillusionment, after the high hopes, may bring sufficient despair to break up the partnership. In some cases there is what is often called a "honeymoon reaction," "a sense of enormous relief and an uprush of loving feelings" ("*Social Casework in Marital Problems*," Tavistock Publications, Ltd., London, 1955, pp 62, 63). This may provide a most useful period of relief from bitter conflict and enable some mutual confidence to be restored, but it may also be used by one or both clients to evade the difficult and possibly painful process of exploring deeper sources of conflict. It is important for the counselor to be aware of this, and to attempt to keep sufficient contact and rapport with the partners, so that they, or a least one of them, may feel able to carry on with the counseling.

In many cases, however these conflicting role perceptions and expectations will not be reconcilable in this way, because they depend on deeper and largely hidden or "unconscious" attitudes, which are so much imbedded into the structure of the clients' personalities that they are accepted uncritically as "reasonable." These hidden factors can generally become revealed through the reactions of each client to the many kinds of interaction described in the interviews if the counselor can make suitable and acceptable "clarifying questioning comments," and this further clarification will generally constitute the next stage in the counseling process.

2. THE CLIENT'S HABITUAL ATTITUDES AND RESPONSES

We have referred to the fact that as the client's narrative proceeds, helped by the counselor's accepting and questioning comments, the counselor will gradually perceive a kind of pattern as it is progressively revealed to him. He regards it as tentative, and continually open for correction or modification as he feels further into the client's attitudes.

A fairly obvious part of this pattern, somewhat wider in scope than the specific role perceptions and expectations in the marital relationship is made up of the client's habitual attitudes and responses. As these are revealed during the interviews the counselor can help the client to clearer awareness of them by "reflecting" them back to him in a manner and tone of voice which show acceptance of them and a desire to understand the client's feelings more fully.

For example, with the interviewing of Betty and Frank already discussed to some extent, Betty might have made several statements which could be summed up in the expression, "If he really loved me he wouldn't mind doing things in the home the way I want them done, would he?" This looks like a habitual attitude which invests "love" with a rather possessive demanding quality inconsistent with the democratic principle of "autonomy" and respect for other people's freedom—even one's marital partner's freedom. How is the counselor to deal with this comment of Betty's, remembering that she is probably unable at the moment to see her habitual attitudes objectively?

If he faced her directly, even if not bluntly, with the statement, "But you can't use love to make people do what you want them to do!" it would probably put Betty's back up and make it even more difficult for her to see her attitude objectively. A type of comment which might be more illuminating to her is, "You feel that those who love you should do what you want them to do?" If she says "yes," it would be unwise for the counselor to turn the situation back and ask, "Would you then do that for someone you loved?" for two reasons. First because that is not the criterion of human behavior; we don't do things because someone else would do the same for us but because we think it right to do them. And second because Betty might well say "Yes I would!" and leave the counselor in a "dead end." A better kind of comment might be, "But it seems that others may not think of love in quite the same way, can you allow for that?" This will give her something to go on pondering over if she doesn't gain insight at that time.

This clarifying process demands considerable patience and tact, and a high standard of empathy, but the general attitude and method of handling is more likely than any other to help the client to growing insight into any destructive habitual attitudes and responses. But there are deeper factors still which may need to come to light if those habitual attitudes are to be overcome. As suggested in the last example there are uncritically accepted assumptions about life, about people, and about the client's own self which have had a lot to do with the formation of the habitual attitudes, and unless these are realized and corrected it may be difficult to change the habitual attitudes.

Linked up with any uncritical assumptions and often dominating them are the person's emotional needs, and his ways of seeking fulfillment of them. For example a client may show indications of a deep need for everyone to agree with him in everything, or for everyone to "understand" him. This constitutes the next stage of clarification.

3. THE CLIENT'S UNCRITICAL ASSUMPTIONS, EMOTIONAL NEEDS, AND WAYS OF SEEKING THEIR FULFILMENT

Although this has been described as distinct from habitual attitudes for purposes of discussion, in actual practice these characteristics of the client will probably be clarified as they emerge without any real distinction. But a person's emotional needs are often deeply imbedded in his personality, well below the level of his awareness, and they may need more patience and skill from the counselor if they are to be helped into awareness. The counselor's own recognized emotional needs may also have a significant influence, often a destructive one, on the counseling process, and it is therefore necessary to give some special consideration to this set of factors in the client's attitudes and conduct.

For example in further interviews with Frank it may appear that he feels quite strongly that he should have no responsibility for any kind of "domestic" responsibility, and as the counselor discusses this attitude further with him he may show some indications of a deep emotional need for "mothering," and the counselor may help to clarify this by some such comment as, "You've felt a bit disillusioned lately at Betty's neglect of your comfort?" Then the interview might proceed as follows:

F. Yes, she used to be quite different when we were first married, she used to anticipate most of my needs, but now I come nowhere, I just earn the money.

C. And you don't feel so happy about it?

F. Well, I had hoped for a bit more thoughtfulness, even though I know she has a lot more on her plate than she had in the early days. I come home tired after a trying day at the office, and I just want to relax and be myself and be fussed over a bit. But I'm fussed over the wrong way, I'm expected to turn to and mend the cupboard door, and keep the kids occupied while Betty gets the table laid.

c. You have the feeling that you're entitled to a bit more consideration after all the hard work you've done at the office. It would help if Betty just let you sit down and relax, and if she brought you something to drink before dinner?

F. Yes, that's exactly what I mean; she used to do that when we were first married, just as my mother used to do it before that. She says now she just hasn't got time with the kids having to be fixed up for bed and with everything else, but I can't see why I should be the one to be left out. As I said, I come nowhere, I just earn the money!

It appears that Frank has little if any insight as yet into his need for continued "mothering," and the counselor might fail to bring him to a more objective view by a direct approach in such a situation. He will probably do better by taking the cue from Frank and going still further back to Frank's relationships in his earlier life, particularly with his mother and father. As before this next "stage" in the clarification is only distinguished from the earlier ones for the purposes of discussion, and in actual practice there need generally be no definite line of cleavage, especially when the client's remarks provide any good opening for deeper exploration. So in this case the interview would move straight on to an exploration of possible reasons for Frank's emotional need for "mothering," so that he might have the opportunity of gaining insight into the situation.

4. THE CLIENT'S BACKGROUND PERSONAL "CONDITIONING"

It is generally agreed that one of the most influential of all factors in the deeper attitudes and feelings of people is the kind of "conditioning" they received in their childhood, particularly in the earliest years of their home and family life. Most of any person's emotional needs have their origin in these early experiences and relationships, and the earlier the needs and assumptions are laid down the more "unconscious" they are likely to be. So almost all marriage counseling for any but the most superficial disorders will need to include some consideration of the early background of each client. As we have seen in the case of John and Mary at the beginning of this book it may be helpful to hear each client's feelings and ideas about the in-laws as well as their own parents, and in this way the counselor may obtain a kind of "two dimensional view" of the early background of both clients, so that he can then help each client to relate present attitudes to early background.

The last part of the interview with Frank might be continued in some such manner as this:

C. Your mother used to be pretty good at anticipating all your needs?

F. Yes, I suppose I was the only pebble on the beach, you see Dad died when I was about 10, and he fortunately left her well enough off, and she didn't have to go out to work. She looked after me like a prince, I didn't have any real duties at home, and I suppose it wasn't very good for me really. We had a married couple who looked after the whole place and they were there until a few years ago.

C. And then, when you married, Betty took over looking after you in the way your mother had done?

F. That's one of the things that attracted me to her, she

was always so thoughtful, and she anticipated every need of her parents, her mother refused to stand in the way of Betty's marriage although she was going through a difficult time emotionally then. But she puts her oar in far too much now, and Betty takes too much notice of her. The result of all this is that I've got to look after myself most of the time, and I don't think it's good enough.

C. Could it be that you feel the need for a kind of "mothering" from your wife?

F. Well, I suppose it could, but why not? Shouldn't a wife who loves her husband try to meet his needs to some extent?

C. And his demands too?

F. I didn't think there was much difference between my needs and my demands.

C. Then you need the "fussing over" as well as demand it?

F. Well, I suppose I can get on without it—I've been getting on without it lately at any rate. Yes, I think I'm beginning to see your point, that I've felt the lack of it mostly because I had so much of it from Mom. Perhaps Betty shouldn't have fussed over me so much at the beginning of our marriage, and I might have come to earth sooner. Actually you know we've each been doing a lot of demanding on one another, and I think I can see now that we've each dug our heels in hard against them. In my case I've felt I had to protect what was left of my individuality that way, and I suppose Betty dug her heels in for the same reason.

C. If, as you feel, each of you has been digging your heels in mainly to resist possible demands, would the best answer be in the direction of cutting our demands on one another?

F. I suppose it would if we could do it, but does that

mean that we would just have to put up with all kinds of inconveniences in silence?

c. What would you think about that? What would a good partner do in such circumstances?

f. I suppose he would tell the other one how he feels and appeal for cooperation. But then I've often appealed to Betty, and she just says she can't do it, and then I get sore. So how can that do much good?

c. If you get sore when she says she can't do it, can you really call it an appeal, or is it really a demand well disguised as an appeal, a wolf in sheep's clothing?

f. I hadn't thought of it quite like that—but I think I'm beginning to see what you mean. If you're not willing to accept "no" for an answer it's really a demand, no matter how like an appeal it may sound. Is that what you're getting at?

c. Well yes, that's what I had in mind, you've got hold of the real difference between an appeal and a demand.

It is obvious here that the exploration of Frank's background personal "conditioning" has brought him to the achievement of some insight into his proneness for dictatorial demands, and the discussion has in this case moved on by its own momentum to further clarification about the difference between appeals, which are helpful in a partnership, and demands, which may be destructive. This approach, through insight into why he wants to make demands, will be more likely to help Frank to stop doing so than any superficial lecture on the futility of demands in a democratic marriage. It may be that the same kind of opportunity may come to help Betty to gain insight into her demanding attitudes and to make some changes in them.

This discussion with either Frank or Betty may lead on to some consideration of helpful attitudes in the face of persisting demands from the other partner. In Frank's case the discussion might possibly go on in some such manner as this:

F. But that's all very well, suppose I stop demanding and become an appealing husband, what do I do when Betty makes demands on me? Wouldn't that make it a rather one sided affair?

C. In questions of this kind do you think the best approach would be to start with some of the facts of life as we know them, and work from there?

F. I'm not quite sure how that applies, the demands are certainly "facts of life," but how can we work from there?

C. Would you agree that one of the facts of life which applies to this is that Betty has, in common with all of us, what we might call the right of free speech; that if she wants to demand the world she is at liberty to do so—and you are equally at liberty to decline to comply with it?

F. But that's pretty much what I've done, isn't it?

C. Have you accepted her right to demand anything, or have you got sore about it and made her feel her right to free speech threatened?

F. Ah! Now I'm beginning to see the point; if I can accept other people's right to demand, and quietly exercise my own right to disappoint them, then we can agree to differ without any great trouble. That seems to have possibilities. I shall have to try it out a bit more with Betty and see how it goes.

Notice how the counselor tries to handle the interview in such a way that the client gradually works out the helpful insights himself, helped at times by "creative questions." This is much better as a rule than any attempt to offer the informa-

tion to him in the form of dogmatic statements, because he is
more likely to accept the ideas he works out himself and still
more to remember them. He is also more able to work out
future decisions on a basis of the facts of life because of this
experience of doing so.

5. THE PERSONALITY TYPES OF THE CLIENTS

During the interviews with each client the counselor will
be gradually gaining some perception of the type of personality
shown by them. This has considerable bearing on many of
their reactions to one another, and also on the essential process
of building a more harmonious relationship, and as the con-
selor comes to realize something of this inner personality type
he becomes better able to act as a mediator between them.

The counselor may come to see how rigid or flexible either
personality may be, and he may make some assessment in his
own mind of whether either personality is of the introvert or
extrovert type, the suspicious "schizoid," the over-dramatic
"hysteric" type, or the very particular "obsessional" type. He
may see evidences of any of the neurotic, psychotic or psychopathic reaction types in one or both clients. It is not his
business as a marriage counselor to make any very accurate
assessment of these psychic patterns, that is a task that is often
difficult enough for a psychiatrist, and much more appropriate for him to attempt than for the counselor.

The counselor, however, needs to have some awareness of
the indications of these manifestations so that he can avoid
persisting with a problem which needs expert professional
help, and make a sensible and appropriate referral as early as
possible. Such referral does not demand any accurate assessment by the counselor, but rather the belief that there are
sufficient indications of such deeper elements to warrant
psychiatric consultation. It is then for the psychiatrist to assess

the conditions and if necessary and acceptable to arrange for the appropriate treatment.

Another important service which the counselor may be able to offer in many cases of marital disorder arising from gross incompatibility of personality type is in the helping a less deeply disturbed partner to cope with the more deeply disturbed one, whether or not under psychotherapy. Some of the indications by which the neurotic, psychotic and psychopathic personalities can be recognized have already been discussed in the section dealing with contributive factors in marital disorder, and some of the ways of helping a bewildered partner to cope with difficult situations will be dealt with in a later section.

It may be emphasized that any "diagnosis" arrived at by the counselor is not stated to either client, that is not the counselor's function. It is kept in his mind as a tentative assessment, continually open to further testing, and used to help in the counselor's handling of the situation in his subsequent interviews with either of the partners or with both of them together.

For example, if one partner consistently dramatized everything and the other one shows perplexity at the apparent irrationality of such attitudes and responses, the counselor might help in the clarification by some such remark as, "You notice that she seems to exaggerate everything and to make far more of things than you would think appropriate. Could it be that she is somehow built that way, that that's her nature?" When the client comes to some acceptance of that possibility the counselor might then put it to him that if she is built that way he might accept her as she is and not take her dramatizations quite so literally. There may well be some opportunity to go into the husband's tendency to take such things so literally, and to open up for him some insight into his possibly obsessional personality, which may have been initially attracted by his wife's dramatizations.

A more difficult problem is that of delusional manifestations, for example when a husband is deeply troubled about his wife's completely unwarranted accusations of infidelity. Here again it is not for the counselor to make diagnoses to either of them, but rather to help each to deal with the problem from his own or her own standpoint. In the early interview with the wife, for example, he might say, "You feel sure your husband is being unfaithful, even though he denies it and you only have indirect evidence for it?" and when the counselor feels that there may be a delusional element in this he might set out to try to induce the client to have some specialist advice.

With the bewildered husband in such a case the counselor might say something like this, "You find that all your emphatic and repeated assurances of your innocence are utterly useless. Would it be worth trying to allow your wife to think and say anything she likes about you to you, and to let your life and your attitudes speak for themselves?" The counselor might add the suggestion that the most helpful attitude to his suspecting wife is that of acceptance of her feelings, however irrational they may seem, in the assumption that she can't help having them. This "agreeing to differ" without hostility on his part may at least preserve some stability in an impossible situation while further help is being sought. This can be done without "labeling" anyone.

To summarize what has been considered so far in the interviews, we began with the establishment of rapport through the encouragement of unburdening on the part of the client and response to the expressed feelings rather than to the facts in the narrative on the part of the counselor. When the feelings have been as fully poured out as the client is disposed to do, the counselor sets out to discern, and to clarify with the client, such underlying influences as role perceptions and expectations in marriage, habitual attitudes and responses, uncritical assumptions, emotional needs, and ways of seeking their fulfilment, background personal "conditioning," and personality type. This may go on with each client separately, often over the same period, but at certain points, and under certain conditions, it may be most helpful, with the consent of both partners, to have one or more interviews with the two of them together. This will be discussed later, remembering that it may happen at any earlier stage of the interviewing.

6. FURTHER CLARIFICATION IN THE "RELATIONSHIP" AREA

As the interviews proceed, either with the partners separately or together, certain specific questions will inevitably come up and need further clarification, and the first group of these to be dealt with are those in the inter-personal or "relationship" area. The most important aspects of the marital relationship which may come under discussion are the sexual, the personal, the parental and the social relationships, and they will be discussed in that order, after which some attention will be given to the question of what goal is being aimed at.

a. *The sexual relationship* is a very common area of marital conflict, as we have already seen in the discussion of contributory factors in marital disorders. In many cases the sexual difficulty is not immediately disclosed, but is hidden behind a "façade" of personal touchiness and "unreasonableness" on the part of the wife, or apparent indifference or infidelity on the part of the husband. As the rapport becomes better the sexual frustrations or conflicts are often expressed, or the counselor may be provided with an appropriate opening for a question about either partner's feelings about the sexual relationship. As already suggested in discussion of contributory factors it is generally impossible to consider the sexual relationship apart from the personal relationship or from the inner personality structure and "conditioning" of the partners.

Whatever the counselor's ideas may be about the meaning and significance of sexual intercourse between human beings, it is necessary for him to listen to the feelings and attitudes of the partners about this important part of their relationship. The aim of counseling is to help them to a mutually satisfying total relationship, rather than to "educate" them "up" to any concept of it, no matter how good, that the counselor may have. For example, if the husband is constantly demanding, much will depend on whether the wife can willingly accept his demands, and if she is happy to do so there seems no justification for the counselor to suggest any other attitude unless asked to do so.

In most cases in which this subject comes up for serious discussion in counseling, however, there is enough painful conflict for a definite review of attitudes to be necessary, and this can only be done on a basis of some workable concept of the meaning and significance of sexual union. Many people have the vaguest ideas of this at the time of marriage and with the normal differences between male and female attitudes to sex they find themselves increasingly at cross purposes after marriage.

If we accept the democratic concept of the dignity of human personality and the autonomy and freedom that go with it, then it seems clear that sexual intercourse cannot properly be the subject of demand on the one hand, but that it is implicit in the marital undertaking that each partner makes a genuine effort to meet the reasonable needs of the other sexually and in all other respects. But this attempt is surely a matter for the individual conscience of each and not for decision by the other partner. In a sense it is more an obligation to the marital partnership than to the other partner, and the marriage will better be promoted and sustained when each makes a genuine effort, with any help that may be found advisable, to live up to the obligation.

Having made these observations it is perhaps necessary to go a little deeper, and to examine some of the inner feelings associated with sexual intercourse in many men and women. The feelings of men are more direct and even demanding than those of most women. Sex, to men, is often felt as a strong "appetite" which seeks gratification and "conquest." Women have a sexual "appetite" that is less direct, and which generally needs to be "awakened," especially at the beginning. Sexual intercourse to a woman involves considerable self-giving, the urge to which needs to be "won" by love rather than demanded by coercion or taken for granted.

Many men fail to understand that their demands for sex intercourse without setting out to win the self-giving cooperation of their wives constitute a recurring affront to their wives' personalities, and that there are limits to the acceptance of such affronts to human dignity. Many wives in counseling make the rather sad observation, "The only time he's ever at all affectionate to me is when he wants sex." The use of any other person as a means to an end (in this case the gratification of an appetite) would seem to be a denial of the very ideas of human dignity and value for which mankind has been fighting over the centuries, and to which we so easily give "lip service."

This kind of approach on the part of husbands may best be exposed for attention in counseling by "creative questioning" at the appropriate time. For example when it is brought out that a husband is regarding sex intercourse as a matter of demand, irrespective of his wife's feelings about it, the counselor might put the question, "Then you feel that your wife should be ready to meet your needs at any time you want her to, regardless of her feelings about it?" In this way, the differing role perceptions can be brought out, and either reconciled by the partners or counseled more deeply by the counselor to elucidate the underlying elements in such attitudes, the habitual attitudes and responses, the uncritical assumptions, emotional needs, and the background "conditioning." This may demand great patience and tact on the part of the counselor, because he is dealing with very deep and highly charged emotions and attitudes which do not lend themselves easily to change.

On the other side the wife who consistently rejects her husband's appeals, or accepts them with hostile compliance may need help in finding out the deeper causative factors in her attitudes. Some of this feeling may arise from inept or crude methods of wooing on the part of the husband, but in many cases there are much deeper factors involved, which may well be related with the early "conditioning," such as an unconscious hatred of men as a result of early experience with a coarse, drunken, cruelly demanding father, or with a tense repressed hostile mother.

When it appears that such conflicting attitudes between the partners extend as deeply as this and do not seem to respond to the general counseling approach it may be advisable for the counselor to consider referral of the partners for deeper psychotherapy, leaving it to the psychiatrist to decide how much therapy he should offer each of them.

While the counseling or psychotherapy is progressing and in cases where it appears that no further counseling or psychotherapy is justified or desired, some help can still be given through examination of the underlying aims of the partners in this area of their lives. Are they, for example, looking for perfect sexual union, something which seems to be beyond the reach of the majority of married couples? Do they on the other hand regard inefficiency in the performance of sexual intercourse as a reflection on their masculinity or femininity? To help the partners to "come to earth" and learn to accept, at least for the time, the best that can be obtained, even if it is not at all comparable with what they had hoped for and expected, may bring about enough release of tension to open the door to a steady improvement in the sexual relationship. This is often found in the case of recently married young people, and if they can even accept the pleasure of being together when the successful conduct of sexual intercourse is beyond their power, the situation may be kept from deteriorating while the necessary counseling and the time for adjustment can be obtained.

As we have seen the sexual and the personal relationships in marriage are closely inter-related. Disturbance of either will inevitably have some upsetting effect on the other. But the personal relationship is generally easier to control than the sexual, and even temporary personal acceptance of sexual difficulties which seem unable to be controlled or overcome by "will power" will make for a more appropriate "atmosphere" for the sexual relationship to develop into greater harmony.

One example of a controllable sexual relationship which can improve the personal relationship in marriage is in the attitude of the partners to sexual intercourse after a personal quarrel. Here is a situation in which the general attitude of men differs markedly from that of women. A man will often think of sexual intercourse as a gesture of reconciliation after a quarrel, but if he seeks to have it in this way his wife will almost certainly regard this as a deep affront to her personality. She will probably be glad to accept it after the personal reconciliation has been achieved, as an expression of their regained unity and not as a means to its achievement. If husbands can be helped to understand this they may save a great deal of misunderstanding and further conflict. Otherwise the husband will seek intercourse in good faith, and then when his wife objects, also in good faith, he will quite wrongly accuse her of obstinacy, and that will increase her resentment and the quarrel will deepen. Sexual intercourse is not appropriately regarded as a means of reconciliation, and its use for that purpose is often merely a way of escaping an honest personal apology.

Another disturbance of the sexual relationship which is quite controllable is what is termed "coitus interruptus," the sudden drawing away of the husband before the emission of semen in an attempt to avoid the risk of impregnating his wife. This may not be related spontaneously in the counseling, at least during the earlier interviews, and it may be necessary for the counselor to ask at some appropriate point how the partners feel about family planning and what they are doing about it. This practice "coitus interruptus" is universally regarded as unwarranted and harmful to the nervous systems of both partners, and the emotional strain associated with it often shows itself in symptoms not necessarily related to the practice. It is often carried out because of ignorance, or because of diffidence about seeking proper help in family planning, and when it is revealed in counseling it is important for the counselor to suggest that the partners obtain some reliable help in family planning from a suitable clinic or from their doctor. Such a referral may lead to great improvement in the whole marital relationship.

Similar medical referral may be advisable in a number of other disturbances of the sexual relationship. The complete lack of satisfaction experienced by many women in the sexual relationship may often be helped by good medical or psychiatric attention. When it is accentuated or caused by extremely painful intercourse in young wives it needs expert help immediately or the situation will almost certainly deteriorate.

In the same way when it is caused by deep fear of possible pregnancy it needs immediate help. Another cause of dissatisfaction, faulty conduct of sexual intercourse on the part of the husband, may also be helped by some appropriate advice, preferably by a doctor.

But many cases of dissatisfaction are not relieved by any of these measures, because they are due to much deeper sexual inhibitions, often the product of faulty conditioning of the wife by parents and others. There may be deep hostilities against men in general which are well hidden from the woman's awareness, but which cause all kinds of apparently irrational and obstinately persistent sexual attitudes, such as frigidity and vaginismus, or even latent or overt homosexual attitudes. When there is any indication of such deeper disorders appropriate referral is generally advisable.

The two most common sexual difficulties in men which are found in cases of sexual dissatisfaction in marriage are impotence and premature ejaculation. Each of these is generally a product of nervousness rather than of any physical or chemical inadequacy, and no hormonal treatment is likely to help unless there are definite physical indications of a glandular deficiency. Many cases of premature ejaculation gradually develop to normality if they are accepted with patience, but cases of impotence are generally of deeper origin and need some form of psychotherapy if they are to be brought back to normal. Even with this the results are not always good, especially when there is any indication of latent or overt homosexuality. Referral is generally advisable.

It is essential to give some consideration to certain apparently abnormal accompaniments of sexual intercourse, because they may well come up for discussion in counseling. It is generally felt by those who have made a special study of these that considerable latitude is essential in assessing what is permissible, as long as two fairly fundamental principles are safeguarded. The first of these is that any such sexual conduct that is distressing or distasteful to the partner should be regarded as in need of serious reconsideration, and the second is that any sexual conduct that takes the place of proper sexual intercourse is to be regarded as abnormal. If the counselor bases his handling of such situations on these two principles he is not likely to do any harm in this kind of situation. In any doubt a referral to the partners' own doctor or to a psychiatrist is worth considering.

In any counseling with partners in sexual difficulties the counselor will generally attempt to gain some knowledge of the total background of the situation by getting some idea of the sexual history of the partners. Much of this may come out spontaneously in the stories that each of them give, but the counselor can add to this by some well designed questions when there is an opening for them. He can keep his own mental processes in an orderly sequence by working back from the present to the past. The general history of the present marriage and the sexual attitudes and methods, the number of children and of miscarriages if any, and the feelings of each about them may come first. Then the history of any previous marriages, the conduct of the courtship and engagement period and of any previous love affairs may be discussed, and an opportunity given for an account of anything that may have been a cause of deep regret or disillusionment. Then the attitude of parents and siblings and playmates at school, and the way in which the early introduction to sex was conducted may be reviewed, together with the emotional attitudes of the client to the various manifestations of sex.

The progressively frank discussion of these emotionally charged elements of the situation in the calm accepting atmosphere of counseling will often prove to be an entirely new experience for the client, and it will do much to overcome many of his bewilderments and fears and to bring a growing release from his emotional conflicts and tensions. Even when there are deeply repressed elements, which need psycho-therapy if they are to be adequately dealt with, the experience of counseling will provide an important part of the therapy, and may even help the clients to a point at which they can go on developing themselves without specialist help. Much will obviously depend on how naturally and comfortably the coun-selor is able to handle the sexual aspects of the clients' nar-ratives, and counsellors need to be at ease in their own per-sonalities in this field if they are to be adequate for the work.

Finally in this discussion of the sexual relationship it might be suggested that at its best human sexual intercourse can be regarded as a complete abandoned self-offering of each to the other as an expression of outgoing unselfish love, a re-enactment together of the partners' "one-flesh-ness" in the marriage relationship, through which it can be progressively deepened and the partners brought to an ever closer union. If it can be accepted in this way there will be less desire to de-mand and more willingness to offer. There will also be more regular personal attention to the quality of love which the regular sexual intercourse seeks to express, and in this way the partners will be much more likely to grow together to greater maturity in their total relationship.

Such a "sacramental" view of sexual intercourse should be at least offered to all young people before marriage and fully discussed with them, so that they are clear in their minds about it. The satisfaction of appetite is in no way disregarded, but it is not then the primary motive for this deeply signifi-cant action, through which it is hoped to nourish and strengthen the loving bond between husband and wife; so that their union can weather all the storms to which marriage, more than ever in these days, is exposed. While ministers may well delegate the work of explaining the physical aspects of sexual intercourse, and even some of the emotional aspects of it, to doctors, it would seem that the Church has a solemn duty and an equally solemn privilege, to offer this deeper spiritual aspect of it to all candidates for marriage, and to people who may seek the counsel of ministers after marriage for any difficulty in their sexual relationships.

b. *The personal relationship.* Professor John Macmurray once described human relationships as of three kinds: instrumental, organic and personal. An instrumental relationship is one in which a person is regarded and used as an instrument, a means to an end. An organic relationship is one in which the participants are related through common membership of a group, and the purpose of the relationship is for the promotion of some sectional common interest. A trade union, a professional association and an employers' federation are examples of this kind of relationship. A personal relationship is one that is self-justifying, it exists for its own sake, although it may fall apart if no common activity or purpose emerges to express the relationship and thereby nourish and strengthen it.

Each of these human relationships may be at the heart of a particular marriage and the bond between husband and wife may change from any one to any other of them. But in counseling we are mainly concerned, not so much with the type of relationship as such, but with the elements of marital conflict, in this case those applicable to the personal relationship. The type of relationship is here important insofar as it is an element in the conflict.

Four common types of conflicts in the personal relationship found in marriage counseling will be discussed, hostility, indifference, dictatorship and dependency. They are often interrelated with one another, but for purposes of discussion they will be dealt with separately.

Hostility is a universal human emotion and there is no human relationship into which it does not enter to some extent. Married couples who boast that they have "never had a quarrel in thirty years of marriage" have generally refused to face the inevitable hostilities. Some married couples who have gone into marriage with the "pipe dream" of the "live happily ever after" phantasy, may be deeply disillusioned by the first expression of real hostility, and may come to the impulsive conviction that their marriage is doomed. They need to be helped to the awareness that love can never be quite "100%"; that even though one may love another person deeply there are times when there is intense hostility against him. What matters most in marriage is not so much the fact of hostility but the extent to which for any reason it is threatening the stability of the marriage or injuring the children.

Hostility may show itself in all kinds of ways, disparaging criticism, belittling, sarcasm, slander, malicious actions, sulking, disloyalty, twisting everything so as to put the "blame" on the other, physical violence, and other forms of mental and physical cruelty. In the marital situation the whole problem becomes so complicated by the mixture of action, reaction, and further retaliatory and protective devices as to be very difficult for anyone to disentangle. But it is not the counselor's task to judge such issues, but rather to provide the atmosphere in which the differences and the hostilities can be openly faced and worked out by the partners if they are willing to do so.

In such working out it is important to distinguish between the "wounds" which come from direct injury; physical or mental cruelty; and those which arise from frustrated expectations which may have been unreal and unwarranted. The husband who expects another "mother" and finds himself with a "wife" may be very hostile at his wife's failure to live up to "mother," but he has somehow to come to terms with reality.

As we have seen previously the most important task of the counselor in handling hostility is to give it sufficient chance to be expressed by each partner in a fully accepting atmosphere; and then to work backward from the hostile feelings to the assumptions about life, about people, and about the client himself (or herself) on which the feelings may be based. In the clarification of hostility it may be that the partners will gain some insight into the distinction between acceptance of the partner's feelings and the nonacceptance of his actions. There's no reason to expect that all that any partner does will be acceptable to the other, but there is a vital difference between "I don't like what you're doing because of so and so" and "You mustn't do that." The first of these is a perfectly warranted expression of attitude, which does not constitute an interference with human freedom, while the second is a threat to human autonomy which is only justified when the unacceptable conduct may cause some oppression or injury to the partner or the children.

In many cases of hostility which come to the counselor the partners each accuse the other of doing something "wrong," when in fact the conflict is often in terms of "difference" rather than "right and wrong." The counselor can often help to clarify these conflicts by asking the appropriate question, "Is it really that your wife (or husband) is wrong in doing this or that you have quite different ideas about it?" "Is it that what seems so wrong to you may not seem wrong to your partner?" Such questions bring some fresh thought to matters and ideas which had been taken for granted. Of course there are some things that are in fact wrong in the sense that they are against the law, or that they are unjustifiably injurious to the marriage, the partner, or the children; and in such cases the offending partner may be faced with the question of the consequences or possible consequences of his actions and the extent to which the other partner will feel disposed to put up with them. In this way the conflict will at least be brought into the open, where it may be possible to deal adequately with it.

When two partners can learn to deal reasonably adequately with hostility in each other they will have reached a good level of emotional maturity, and will be able to help each other greatly in any outbursts of hostility which are always possible in marriage. It is a strange fact of experience that many husbands and wives who are able to be charming, gracious and well-behaved with everybody else are repeatedly hostile, ill-mannered, and very ill-behaved with their own partners and their children, as if their main rebellion is against the marriage and family bond, or the obligations of marriage. This may also be helped by clarification in the counseling.

Indifference is another very common disturbance of the personal relationship of marriage to come up for consideration in marriage counseling. It is also apparently very common in many marriages for which no counseling is sought. It is often a slow insidious "disease" of marriage, and it shows itself in many different ways. There may be a lack of common interests and cooperative activities, a lack of interest in or even awareness of the feelings, the needs or the rights of the partner or the children, or there may be a neglect of the essential responsibilities concerning the house or the financial necessities. Each may gradually come to go his own way and live like boarders in the same house without any real companionship.

Indifference is a less dramatic, but a far more serious disorder of marriage than hostility, and a much more difficult one for the partners to deal with, because the necessary motivation has generally been more or less destroyed. While hostility is the emotional "opposite" of love and is apt, like all emotions, to be changeable; indifference is the "opposite" of the "goodwill" aspect of love, the sustained and sustaining bond of marriage, and it is more likely to be an established attitude, less open to change. When indifference comes into the marriage the deep emotional needs of the partners for affection and companionship are frustrated, and the stage is set for strong urges for either of them to seek the fulfilment of such needs elsewhere. This of course will tend to make the situation still more difficult and complicated.

When indifference or withdrawal of companionship are discovered in the counseling the counselor will seek to discover and to help the partners to understand something of why it came about. It may be that the original decision to marry was based on inadequate foundations or motives, and then the partners need to work out their ideas of how they can find ways of building better on what resources they have or can develop. It may be that one or both have personal inadequacies that may be overcome to some extent with patient help, or that their marital relationship has become upset by misunderstandings or failures, or that pressures from their environment have proved overwhelming. Any or all of these possible determining factors will need to be explored in the counseling, together with their relationships as children with the significant people in their lives.

One specific kind of indifference merits particular attention, the fairly common reaction of wives when they return home after childbirth. The emotional strain of pregnancy and the confinement, and the intense stirring of the maternal instinct through contact with and nursing of the eagerly anticipated baby may leave little emotional energy for a time for her to offer to the husband. In some cases, of course, when the baby is not greatly wanted, there may be still more emotional strain, with the addition of feelings of guilt and frustration, together with some apprehensiveness about the mother's ability to carry the job of parenthood through satisfactorily. In either case the newly returned mother of the first, and even more of the second and third child, may feel a kind of indifference to the advances and even the needs of her husband. If he does not understand this it may well bring considerable hostility on his part from the "injustice" of being "treated like that when he has been denied some of the normal relationships during the later months of his wife's pregnancy." If the husband can accept his wife's temporary indifference, even though he may find it hard to understand it, and can support her in the difficult task of settling down to a radically changed household, with a new baby and sometimes also with one or more jealous toddlers, she will generally negotiate the readjustment that is necessary without much delay, and their personal relationship will be strengthened through the experience of going through the difficult period together.

Situations of this kind may be very much more difficult when they are complicated by any "parent fixation" on the part of either husband or wife. Unless this can be faced and dealt with the indifference will more likely become fixed, and the barriers will grow steadily more impenetrable.

Dictatorship is almost invariably found in marital conflict, and it is sometimes one of the most influential elements in the disorder. It is generally rationalized in some way, and it tends to stir up reactions in the "victim" which only make matters worse. Behind the dictatorial attitudes are often such intra-personal inadequacies as immaturity, perfectionism, deep insecurity and feelings of inferiority, and other kinds of neurotic and even psychotic personality. In other cases it may arise as a reaction to dictatorship in the partner, in the conviction that the only way to guard against being overwhelmed by a dictator is to do the same oneself. In this way it is often found that each partner can quite logically accuse the other of being dictatorial.

The external manifestations of dictatorship will vary greatly with the type of personality of the "dictator." There may be aggressive expressions, such as domineering, tyranny, shouting, physical cruelty or violence, financial tyranny, and a rooted and well rationalized determination to "make the other one over" to an arbitrary pattern in the mind of the "dictator." The aggressive attitudes are often carried over into the sexual relationship, with threats of all kinds of retaliation if the demands are not fulfilled.

On the other hand there may be less openly aggressive expressions, such as nagging and "needling," sulking, masochistic "suffering," or even actual sickness. At times there may be even demands on the partner to feel in a particular way, for example when a husband willingly goes with his wife to some function he doesn't enjoy at all, simply out of love for her and the desire to do things with her, and she is hurt because he didn't enjoy the function.

The first task of the counselor is to help the dictatorial person to a realization that in fact he is demanding, whether or not he may feel there are adequate reasons for doing so. This is often surprisingly difficult, especially in the case of men, who may still have deep in their minds the largely obsolete concept that marriage is a male-dominated affair. It is common for a husband or wife to make a clear and definite demand and in the next breath deny completely that any demand has been made! There may be such a comment as "All I ask is that —," or a statement that he is not demanding, but only appealing to the partner.

In such cases the question, "Can you tell me the difference

between an appeal and a demand?" will generally bring some deep thought, and the most common answer will be in some such terms as "It depends on what way it is put. A demand is put in forceful terms and an appeal in reasonable terms." This of course is not necessarily true, many demands can be put in most reasonable appealing terms, but they are none the less demanding. The partners need to see that the real difference is that an appeal is willing to take "no" for an answer, while a demand, however appealingly put, is not willing to take "no" for an answer. Once this is realized and accepted the partners will have this whole question much better clarified in their minds, and there will be fewer demands in most cases.

It is difficult for many people to accept the idea that we cannot hold people up to their moral (as distinct from their legal) obligations. We can express disapproval, and make our own adjustment or reaction to what is being done, but we cannot abolish the "autonomy" or self-government which is the very core of democratic society, for which men and women have fought and died over the centuries. Bernard Shaw once made the penetrating observation that "when all the other autocracies have vanished from the world, the last autocracy left will be the family—usually governed by the worst disposition in it."

The demanding person then, unless the partner is an excessively compliant person, will need to come to the realization that we can only seek to win other people's cooperation; that any cooperation gained by coercion, bribery or trickery is only superficial and generally worth very little. The "victim" of demands may come to the realistic insight that it is not necessary to prevent the demands from being made, that would constitute a denial of free speech. Neither is it necessary to respond by attempted dictatorship, that leads to stalemate or deeper conflict. It is possible to grant the other person the privilege of demanding what he likes, and reserving the natural freedom to comply or not to comply. The "victim" might respond in some such manner as "You want me to do so and so, but I'm sorry, I don't feel it's right for me to do that, and I shall have to disappoint you." This is an application of the simple democratic principle of "live and let live." We can do what we feel to be right, not necessarily what we want to do, and not what somebody else thinks is right for us. To stand firm on one's own convictions in this way, while granting others the privilege of thinking and saying what they like about it, would seem to be the only realistic democratic way of living, domestically or socially.

When someone disapproves deeply of any action it behooves us to give genuine consideration to that attitude, and if possible to find out why it is being held, rather than to be obstinately fixed in what we have decided. We can often learn from our severest critics, and the very fact of giving serious consideration to any such criticism or demand will do much to preserve the relationship. We can accept such criticism more calmly when we remember that it is the duty of a partner to express his ideas on matters affecting the partnership in any way, rather than to be a "silent partner," especially rather than to harbor hostile feelings in such matters.

It is possible therefore to deal with many disagreements by accepting the partner's feelings on the matter involved, and accepting his conduct within the law, but feeling free to express one's own feelings about it. In such attitudes as this the way is open for the constructive use of disagreements and conflicts. It is well that this is possible, for there will inevitably be many conflicts in marriage and family living.

Such handling of conflicts can be of real help in some particular kinds of conflict, such as those found in "mixed marriages," and those with "in-laws," or with other people such as employers and friends.

Dependency, the fourth of the disruptive elements in the personal relationship of marriage, is also normally found to some extent in practically every marriage. Aristotle is credited with the observation that "the man who can do without his fellows is either a beast or a god!" We are inter-dependent rather than independent, and the question that matters in this aspect of marriage counseling is the degree of dependency and its effect on the marital relationship.

As with the other elements we have considered, dependency can show itself in many different ways. One partner may be an inveterate "leaner" on the other, and appear to have little or no capacity to stand on his or her own feet. This dependency may show itself as intense possessiveness or jealousy, or in persistent demands on the partner of the different kinds we have been considering.

When such expressions of dependency come into counseling it is for the counselor to try to discover as many of the background reasons for the dependency as possible, because the best growth will come when the causative factors can be understood and if possible dealt with. He will also need to make some tentative assessment of the possible resources for growth in the dependent person, and of the attitudes and resources of the partner through which the situation may be given time and opportunity for positive development. Some actual suggestions may be necessary for a dependent person, as long as they are not offered in such a way as to increase the dependency or to divert it onto the counselor. For example if a wife seems quite helpless in the management of the home and in such essential matters as cooking, the suggestion of a definite attempt to gain some training in these things would seem to be valid. The counselor will put such suggestions in the "creative questioning" form, such as "Do you think it would help if you could go and get some domestic training at one of the domestic science schools, or from some friend or relative?" In this way the initiative is left to some extent with the client, and necessity can still remain for him or her "the mother of invention"—and of growth.

The partner of the excessively dependent person may need some help in the acceptance of the amount of dependency that seems inevitable at any stage in the counseling progress, because any great impatience or hostility might well reduce the dependent person to despair, and make the whole project more difficult or even impossible. To live with a dependent person may require considerable judgment regarding how much can be left to him to do, even at the risk of domestic untidiness for a time, and considerable patience to give time and sufficient encouragement for development. But with reasonable care it is generally possible for two partners to develop to a remarkable extent in such cases, particularly if any accessible underlying factors, such as previous over-mothering, can be faced and worked through in the counseling.

c. *The parental relationship* in this part of the discussion means the particular part of the husband-wife relationship which is concerned with their mutual function as parents. Many areas of deep conflict may come up in counseling which involve this aspect of marriage. Those which will be dealt with may be considered in chronological order.

The first that may arise is premarital pregnancy, with some very deep emotional consequences in each partner. It may be that they decide to marry largely because of the heavy pressure of the respective families, especially that of the girl. In such cases there is great danger of resentment on either side, and such matters are all too often "thrown up" at one or other partner when hostilities arise from any cause. The memory of the premarital intercourse may generate or increase deep suspicions by either husband or wife of the fidelity of the other in later years. Such dangers are lessened when the two young people marry by free mutual consent with the full knowledge that there is another good alternative, the offering of the baby for adoption, even though it may be an agonizing decision for the mother.

In some cases, when a pregnant girl is persuaded or coerced to the participation in an illegal abortion, there are profound effects on her deepest emotions, some of which may not show themselves for many years. When such cases come to the counselor before marriage and he is faced with the decision of the girl to seek such an abortion, it is his duty to make sure at least that she realizes some of the less obvious consequences of what she is considering. It may also be necessary for the counselor to have some discussion with other participants in the whole matter, such as the father of the child and the parents of the two lovers. In this way it may be possible for the impulsive urges of fear and guilt-stricken people to be controlled, and for some rational and honest consideration of the whole situation to be encouraged.

The girl who either hands her baby over for adoption or has it removed by abortion will often be in great need of help, and in many cases the counselor can offer good cooperation to the girl's doctor who may also be offering some help. In this way she may be able to unburden her feelings more fully and come to more radical adjustment, often with the further help of a wise minister. There will then be less danger of permanent wounds to her personality which might otherwise do damage to future marital relationships and future parenthood.

Next, in point of time may come an unexpectedly early pregnancy and parenthood, possibly with quite serious consequences from the point of view of finance and housing. Some good help here may sometimes be given by a social worker, and it often happens that with good counseling ways can be found to help such young people through the difficult adjustment to the unexpected early responsibility of parenthood.

Too many children for the young couple's resources of money, housing and energy may also bring some marital disorder, especially when there are difficulties in the way of effective family planning, either from ignorance or stupidity, or from conscientious objections. In the same way a succession of children coming too soon after one another may have some adverse effects on the partnership as well as on the wife's health. Good counseling in such matters, with possible referral for special help, may bring better conditions and an improvement in the relationship.

At the other extreme a young couple for various reasons may delay parenthood for an unduly long period, and become so well adapted to each other and to a childless marriage that they either give up the idea of parenthood altogether, or find the child or children a hindrance to their previously settled life. This delay or denial of motherhood, either by her own desire or still more by some kind of pressure from her husband, may have quite considerable effects on the wife's emotional attitudes, in ways not obviously connected with the particular frustration. Many doctors have seen a nervous, irritable, restless wife come to a dramatic recovery with the arrival of her own or even an adopted child, even when she was not at all happy about an unexpected pregnancy.

Disagreements about the question of adoption when desires for children of their own have been unfulfilled sometimes appear to be quite a large element in a marital disorder, especially when the wife has a strong maternal instinct and the husband a rooted objection to adoption. The parents of each partner may well have their strong opinions and have no hesitation in expressing them. Counseling which seeks to find any deep underlying factors in such attitudes may help them to find a way through the situation which does no great violence to any of the personal feelings concerned. Many people have vague or distorted ideas about adoption and open discussion in the accepting atmosphere of counseling will often bring more sense of realism to the situation. Husbands don't always realize the depth of the frustration of the maternal instinct in their wives in such cases. In any case of apparent infertility it is of course understood that the partners will have been referred for special medical investigation of the situation.

A common element in marital disorder is the effect on the husband of the arrival of the first or any other child with the consequent change in the balance of the family. There may be deep unconscious vulnerabilities in the husband which are suddenly brought to the surface when a child arrives, and their manifestations appear quite irrational until the deeper elements are realized. The well known situation of the husband who finds mothering in a "maternally minded" wife and feels rejected and jealous when she becomes involved with more natural objects for mothering was described at the beginning of this book. A deeper vulnerability which may occur in a husband is that which stems from his childhood jealousy of a little brother or sister which was punished or belittled by his parents and therefore repressed. In such cases he may have quite "unreasonable" hostility to his new baby, and deep jealousy of any attention his wife gives to perfectly natural mothering of the child. This will be helped greatly when it is brought out in the counseling.

Another kind of conflict affecting the mutual task of parenthood is in the general type of care and discipline of children. This of course is best worked out between the partners either during the engagement period or at least before the arrival of their children, but many couples fail to do this adequately and find themselves in quite serious quarrels about the handling of children. Here again many attitudes of husband and wife come less from "reason" than from deep habitual attitudes which have "carried over" from their own childhood. In counseling their differing rationalizations may well give place to more compatible realistic ideas when each of them is given the chance to relate present feelings to the background experience. Sometimes a referral to a child guidance clinic may be helpful.

d. *The social relationships*. This is a fairly wide field, which may cover such matters as friends, sports and hobbies, business and professional associates, necessities of work (such as travelling or "working back" or "entertaining"), and involvement with church work or other kinds of voluntary social service. Any of these may be brought up in counseling as elements in the trouble, and as in previous cases there are many deeper but more influential factors in most of these problems than are immediately obvious.

In some cases the trouble has been felt from the beginning and then may stem from the fact that one or both of the partners have failed to adapt themselves from a comfortable individualism to the responsibility of marriage. Their "I" has failed to become in any real sense "We." This is a kind of immaturity, often the product of "spoiling" by overindulgent parents in childhood, and such people may enter marriage with the naive idea that they will go on being coddled. They have never been able to develop a sense of responsibility to any but compulsory tasks, and not always even to them. This situation may involve considerable patience on the part of both partners and also of the counselor, because growth of any kind is always slow. The counselor's task, having helped the partners to understand the realities of the situation, is to try to help them hold the marital relationship while the growth and the learning can have sufficient time to produce results.

Sometimes the undue preoccupation of a partner with many old friends of the same sex is a result of latent or even actual homosexuality, and in such cases there will almost always be quite obvious disturbances of the sexual relationship between the partners as well. When there is any indication of the possibility of this kind of trouble a referral is advisable.

Probably most of the social difficulties which are not the result of unavoidable duties are really symptoms of a deeper conflict between husband and wife, a slowly corroding indifference which has gradually made home less attractive and desirable. Many husbands who spend hours "with the boys" on the way home each evening, to the growing resentment of their wives, would come home much more readily if the atmosphere were more attractive. When the wife objects, which she feels quite justified in doing, it only tends to make the husband feel less anxious to come home, and the children suffer from both the absence of their father and the increasing peevishness of their mother.

In such cases it is essential to open up the deeper elements before any worthwhile healing of the marital situation can be expected. To tell such a husband that he ought to take more interest in his wife and his home, and to tell the wife that she ought to make the home more welcoming, will generally leave each of them quite unmoved. They will have had much of this kind of advice from interested relatives, and it will most likely have added to their feelings of despair. When the deeper elements are brought to the surface and many old "festering sores" are faced and dealt with the way may become open for a restoration of the deeper emotional communication and the recovery of mutual affection and confidence, and a new era may well dawn in the marriage. Unless the marriage and the home can be given a high priority in the feelings of each partner the situation will be in danger of such deterioration as we have been considering.

e. *What goal is being aimed at in marriage counseling?* This question is worthy of some consideration because marriage is not a fixed or uniform kind of relationship. There are many kinds of successful marriages, and any counselor who, consciously or unconsciously, seeks to make his own concept of marriage the goal of his counseling will often find himself in difficulties. The very essence of counseling is that the clients are helped to work toward the kind of marital relationship that they find mutually satisfactory, which may be quite different from what the counselor would regard as a good marital relationship.

In emphasizing this it must also be recalled that certain kinds of marital relationship are less stable or more vulnerable than others, and it may be appropriate for the counselor to help any couple to some realization of the possible dangers, so that they can recognize any early indications of trouble and seek any necessary help. A case in point has already been suggested, the maternally minded girl giving a lot of "mothering" to an already "over-mothered" husband, and each of them finding the relationship quite satisfactory. This is of course a very vulnerable kind of marriage if any children are expected in the future, and it would help the partners to prepare for the readjustment if they have some idea of the dangers.

With this kind of reservation it is important for the counselor to keep in his mind the essential fact that his function is to help his clients to better insight into their own and their partners' attitudes and actions so that they can work out with each other the kind of marital relationship that they find most mutually acceptable.

Some idea of the different kinds of successful marriage can

be obtained by thinking of them from the points of view of certain specific categories. For example using domination as a criterion we can see many apparently successful marriages in which the husband is the dominant partner, others in which the wife is dominant, and all grades between the two with varying degrees of domination and cooperation in the different areas of the lives of the partners. As long as the relationship is mutually acceptable these different patterns of marriage can be quite successful.

Another category, which may well overlap with the first, is the manner in which the partners attempt to settle their main differences. Here again we have all variations between the quiet peaceful home and that in which the partners seem to revel in brawls and quarrels, even to the point of shouting and screaming at each other, and yet seem to get on very well together and to form a strongly united front in the face of any external threat or difficulty. Another group of partners find that they can discuss many of their differences openly, but that some of them are "walled off" and kept out of the way in order to preserve peace. This may be vulnerable, but many couples manage to get on well in this way.

A third category, again overlapping with the others, is what may be called the pivot on which the partnership revolves. There are marriages which are mainly governed by the welfare of the children, and the parents seem to delight in submerging themselves for their children's benefit. At the other end of this scale there are marriages in which the children are largely left to look after their own welfare, and the partners put their own affairs first, or possibly they even regard some community activities as of sufficient importance to override everything else. Again any of these marriages can be successful as long as the policy is one of mutual acceptance.

A fourth category is that of general administration, and here there are great variations between the couples who do most things together and have almost all their interests in common and those at the other end of the scale who largely delight in going their separate ways and find great interest in each other's activities. The necessary common interest in such cases is in each other's separate doings, and as long as they agree in this way of administering their partnership it can work well. A still less definite kind of structure which can work very well within its limitations is the "de facto" partnership, in which for some unalterable reason the partners are unable to go through the official form of marriage but find a mutual delight and mutual benefit in the unconventional partnership.

A final category to be mentioned here is that of the varying roles in marriage, from the conventional one of a husband as breadwinner and his wife looking after the home and family, through various kinds of situation in which husband and wife both work and the children are managed largely by a grandmother or a housekeeper, to the occasional situation in which the conventional roles are completely reversed. In this latter case the husband may, for example, have been crippled by poliomyelitis or some other ailment or injury, and may keep an eye on the domestic scene while his wife acts as the breadwinner. Here again each of these patterns can work very well if they are accepted by mutual consent.

There are probably many other categories by which differing patterns of successful marriage can be assessed, even to an occasionally successful "triangular situation." But enough has been suggested to make it clear that marriage is largely what the partners want it to be, and not a rigid or constant pattern imposed by anyone else, especially not by any good counselor.

7. FURTHER CLARIFICATION IN THE "INTRA-PERSONAL" AREA

As we have seen the marriage counselor as such is mainly concerned with offering help in the disturbed relationship between the partners rather than in the inner personality dynamics of either of them. This intra-personal area is much more the province of the psychotherapist, and the marriage counselor as such is not trained to do psychotherapy in this sense.

But it is generally impossible to draw any sharp line between the "relationship" and the "intra-personal" areas in the majority of marital problems that come for help, and if every intra-personal disturbance discovered by the marriage counselor were referred to a psychiatrist there would soon be an oversaturation of the available time and energy of all the psychiatrists in any country.

It is therefore part of the training of marriage counselors, and indeed of social workers, to keep predominantly within their own fields, the marriage counselor within the relationship field and the social worker within the environmental field; but to be able to deal with the less intense and complex elements of their clients' problems which may encroach to some extent into the associated fields. In any such extension they are under an obligation to recognize their limitations and to seek appropriate referral whenever it seems at all advisable or in any case of doubt. In fact many social workers find that their knowledge and experience enable them to use the rapport they gain with clients to help them greatly in their relationships and in their inner personality disorders. In some clinics this is done with the full approval of the psychiatrist in charge. The same spread into related fields cannot altogether be avoided by the marriage counselor.

In an earlier chapter we have considered some of the most common intra-personal factors which can contribute to marital disorder under four headings, ignorance or misinformation, immaturity, illness, physical and mental, and irreligion; and some account has been given of the main indications of these factors and of their possible effects on the marital relationship. We may now consider how the counselor sets out to elicit and to clarify his clients' attitudes and feelings in this area.

Many of the more obvious indications of intra-personal disorders will come out spontaneously in the progress of the counseling, especially as the counselor looks with clients at their role perceptions, their habitual attitudes and responses, their uncritical assumptions and emotional needs, their background "conditioning" and their personality types. By the kind of "creative question" already discussed, asked at the most appropriate point in the discussion to follow out the clients' trains of thought the clarification can continue.

As we saw in the previous section on "further clarification in the relationship area," many intra-personal disorders and distortions will come up so closely interrelated with the relationships that they cannot be separated from them, even if that were desirable. But if the counselor has some kind of orderly arrangement in his own mind he can save himself from confusion of thought and help the client to more ordered thinking too. All of these classifications are mainly for that purpose, and to some extent to assist in orderly description.

When the counselor discovers indications of ignorance or misinformation regarding some significant or potentially significant matter for the marital relationship it is generally best to begin by encouraging the client to further unburdening so that counselor and client may come to a clearer idea of how the client came to think as he did. In this way the client is kept in active participation in the interview, and is more likely to be open to further information and to remember it. The actual information given is also more likely to fit the client's real needs when he has been encouraged to talk out the particular point that has come up.

A client can often be helped to work out many insights of this kind by creative questioning. For example the "perfectionistic" wife might be asked some such questions as this: "If you feel that you must insist on your high standards being lived up to by everyone else in the family, why shouldn't any of the others expect their lower standards to be accepted by you and all the others?" Such a question will possibly start some further consideration of a few of the principles of human relationships.

In other cases some definite appropriate information on matters within the knowledge of the counselor may be given to the client in simple terms, and if necessary repeated on subsequent occasions. It sometimes takes time and repetition for new concepts to take root in a client's mind. The best time for the giving of information is after the emotional tensions and conflicts have had sufficient opportunity to become unburdened, because as we have seen emotion tends to "blind" many people to "sweet reason."

In considering the offering of information the counselor needs to watch for evidences of mental illness, particularly such manifestations as delusions. It is waste of time, and generally more harmful than beneficial, to attempt to "educate" people out of any kind of delusion. A workable approach to such a situation as the assertion that someone is inflicting illness on the client by electricity, is as follows: "You feel you are being attacked in this way, what do you feel you can do about it? What help were you hoping for from me?" It is a relief to some people worried by delusions to find someone who will give them any kind of hearing, instead of the reiterated affirmation that what they think is happening is impossible. Ultimately, when the deluded person has told the counselor that the police, the lawyers, the doctors and the ministers have all "let him down," the counselor may come with him to the suggestion, "Well, if it is as you think, it looks as if you've got to live and do your job in spite of them and call their bluff." It is assumed in all of this discussion that psychiatric help has been sought, and when the situation of such a person becomes unbearable, of actual or potential danger to him or to anyone else, the psychiatrist will arrange appropriate institutional care.

There are many delusional assertions which are completely outside the counselor's available knowledge, such as the repeated accusation by a wife that her husband is carrying on with one or more other women, generally backed by all kinds of plausible but circumstantial "evidence." When this is repeated in session after session, the counselor may be forced to such a question as this: "If you can't accept your husband's repeated assurance that he is 'playing the game' with you, how can I help you in this part of the trouble? It may be that she will need some help in the difficult task of living with the indelible ideas of her husband's "infidelity," even though he too is in constant deep distress at his wife's trouble and his own inability to "get across" to her. He may also need help in coping with a wife who cannot let him alone, and accuses him night and day of "carrying on" with other women.

Another possible and sometimes effective method of dealing with ignorance and misinformation is through books, booklets, pamphlets, and occasionally the provision of lectures. These need to be well chosen with regard to the suitability of the material, the manner and the spirit in which they are presented, and the capacity of the clients to profit by them. The appropriate time for offering such help through literature also needs careful consideration.

When literature or lectures are offered to clients it is well for the counselor to offer them the opportunity of discussing the material in subsequent sessions, encouraging them to mark any particular parts of the material which they may wish to discuss, and also eliciting from them their general impressions of the information that has been offered, and the application of the various matters to their own situation. General and specific information given in books or lectures or pamphlets needs to be applied to the particular feelings and needs of the clients if it is to be of the most practical value. Dealt with in this way it forms a very important part of the counseling process, and it has increased value because it can be taken up and studied at any future occasion if needed. Most if not all marriage counseling agencies keep a supply of printed material for distribution and sale, and also have lists of recommended reading material. Many of them also organize classes of instruction for those who may feel disposed to enroll.

In dealing with apparent immaturity of any kind in either partner the counselor will generally attempt to encourage the client to discuss his earlier background "conditioning," and this has already been dealt with in a previous section. In seeking to find out what kind of relationships existed between the client and significant people in his childhood the question, "How did you get on with your mother (or other person)?" is likely to be answered in such a manner as "Oh all right," which may tend to close the discussion. A more productive approach is through the question, "What sort of person was your mother?" and in answering that kind of question the client will generally bring out many important aspects of his relationship with her. With similar questioning about father, step-parents, aunts, uncles, grandparents, teachers, brothers, sisters, half-brothers and sisters, and "unofficial" uncles and aunts, and friends. As we saw in the first case record in this book it may help to obtain a two-dimensional view of the client's background, from the client himself and from his partner, who will usually have some knowledge of it; and also possibly from anyone else with good knowledge. In such ways as this a fairly complete impression can be gained of the client's "style of life" (as Adler called it), which may help in the further counseling.

An important aspect of immaturity is the "vulnerability" of the client, and his "rigidity" of thought, attitude and behavior. In his unburdening the counselor will gain some idea of what kinds of attitude and behavior in others upset him or stir up hostile reactions in him. The counselor may then be able to look with him behind the vulnerabilities to the uncritical assumptions and emotional needs and other inner factors which have contributed to them. They are better dealt with at this deeper level than at the superficial one.

When there are indications of any form of mental illness the counselor will necessarily consider the advisability of referral, but in some milder and less obvious cases he may be able to help the client to better insight and better relationships. For example many clients show indications of self-hate, self-disparagement or even self-punishment, which may be traceable back to the kind of conditioning which came from their parents. Others will show indications of projection or reaction formation, or other mental processes dealt with in a previous section. These are sometimes open to counseling help, but when at all persistent or severe they generally need psychotherapy.

Any apparently abnormal sexual attitudes or psychopathic manifestations will also bring the counselor to consider referral as long as the marital situation is being threatened or upset by them. Some attempt to find the background factors in the assumption of such attitudes may be justifiable, and occasionally this will make it possible for the client and partner to understand them better and to work out constructive ways of dealing with them.

Certain religious attitudes in one or both clients may appear to cause quite serious conflicts in marriage, and these are often very difficult to deal with because they are at a level of thought which is not altogether open to reason, and are the products of long continued childhood conditioning. But such difficulties are a challenge to mutual tolerance which is supposed to be one of the products of good religion, and the counselor might well try to help the partners to face their religious conflicts on that basis. If they can learn to do this it may develop their religious attitudes towards much greater maturity and practical relevance. In many cases of immature or rigid religious attitudes this may demand very great tact and patience; and a way of handling the situation which comes "not to destroy but to fulfill," and which does not seek to impose any of the counselor's religious attitudes on the clients.

Where the difficulty and conflict is in the kind of religious training which is to be given to the children it may be difficult to find a way through the trouble which is acceptable to both partners. It is much better when such difficulties are anticipated and worked out between the partners before the children come, but when this has not been done the counselor has to make the best of the situation in the face of all the emotional tensions which so often surround it. There is one general principle which may possibly be offered at any appropriate stage in the counseling, that in those cases where the differences are at all great it is better for the children to share the religious attitudes and denomination of their mother, with whom they naturally have closer ties, than those of the father. For children to grow up with religious attitudes at variance with those of their mother involves difficulties and adverse consequences beyond general awareness, and the counselor may feel it incumbent on him to offer this information.

CHAPTER VII

The Arranging and Handling
of Joint Interviews

THE WHOLE QUESTION of joint interviews needs to be considered in relationship with two important facts—first, that nearly all marital disorders have very strong emotional components which by their very nature tend to take control of any discussions and to divert them from any "reasonable" path; and second, that the counselor will be carrying out with the partners something that they may have already tried many times without him, and generally failed to solve their conflicts in doing so.

But the presence of the counselor introduces a very influential element into any such discussion. Each partner will unconsciously as well as consciously relate his attitudes to the counselor in one way or another. He may try to win the counselor's emotional support, and he may well restrain himself from many obviously absurd accusations which he might have made otherwise. From another point of view the counselor brings what can be a vital influence into such joint discussions in that if, say, a husband is deeply hurt in the counselor's presence, the humiliation may put him so much on the defensive that he might not feel able to go on in any but a superficial manner with further counseling.

It seems clear therefore that joint interviews need careful consideration and even more careful and tactful handling if the dangers of excessive wounding on the one hand or of loss of rapport on the other are to be minimized.

In some cases the two partners come together for the first appointment, and it may be helpful to consider some of the possible meanings of this action. As we have seen previously it may mean that they have a mutual willingness to look for a way through their difficulties, and are not aware of any great emotional conflict between them. In other cases they come together because they have the idea that this would be expected of them.

There may however be some deeper reasons for their coming together. For example there may be in one or both of them a deep suspicion that the first one to be interviewed may gain some advantage by "getting in first," which suggests their idea that the counselor is going to act as a kind of judge. There may be a desire to "answer" all criticisms and accusations the moment they are made, coupled with a fear of being discussed "behind their backs."

In most cases when the two partners come together for the initial appointment the counselor will have them both in for the beginning of the interview, and will observe them closely while he is listening to whoever is doing the talking. When there is any indication of emotional tension in one or both, either outwardly expressed or less directly conveyed by sitting silently and looking away from the counselor and the partner, the counselor will generally suggest that it is mostly easier for people to talk freely in the absence of other people, and offer them the opportunity for individual interviews. When put in this way the offer is usually accepted, and it is either left to the partners to decide who shall be first, or the counselor suggests that the one who seems to be least anxious to talk might have the first opportunity. In many cases this person has been a bit overwhelmed by the more active partner, and if sent out may feel even more crushed.

If one of the partners has more difficulty in arranging convenient times for appointments it may be right to have that one in first, and in such cases the partners will often suggest that themselves. But in all cases when both partners come for the first appointment each of them should be given some time alone with the counselor, even if with the second partner it is only a short session which shows acceptance of some feelings and sets the stage for another fuller session within a short time. In this way neither partner is so likely to feel frustrated after summoning up quite a lot of will power to make the initial approach to the counselor. This first contact is, as we have seen, of the greatest importance as the foundation of the counseling relationship.

This section is concerned, however, mainly with the joint interviews which might be arranged by the counselor at some appropriate point in the series of interviews. There are two main reasons for his wishing to arrange such joint interviews.

The first of these is when one or both clients tend to concentrate mainly on the objectionable attitudes and the misdeeds of the other, and seem unable or unwilling to face their own contributions to the disorder. If the counselor just goes on allowing them to talk about their grievances in this way the counseling may well reach a point of "stalemate," unless their unburdening can go on well enough and for long enough for them to gain adequate insight. When this doesn't seem to be possible it may be tempting for the counselor to bring up some point offered by the other one, for example, "Your wife seems to feel rather upset by what she thinks is your cruelty to her." A common answer to such a statement is, "She's exaggerating that, I'm not cruel at all." What is the counselor to do then? Is he to take it up with the wife next time, and say, "Your husband thinks you're exaggerating," which would not be of any help to her or to the counseling because she would deny his remarks with indignation. The counselor cannot become a "tale bearer" without doing a lot of possible harm to the counseling.

When each client persists with accounts of the other's misdeeds and doesn't face any of his own it often helps to seek a joint interview, first asking the consent of each of them, and then asking whether each one would be able to bring up any matters which are distressing them. There are certain essential conditions of successful joint interviews which will be discussed shortly, and when these are fulfilled the counselor may find such an interview very helpful.

Suppose in this joint interview "Mary" brings up her concern at "John's" cruelty. John may then accuse her of exaggeration, and Mary will then say something like this: "But you remember on such and such an occasion when you got really mad with me and you grabbed me by the neck and nearly choked me. I still don't think you realize how you scared and hurt me in your raging temper!"

In many such cases John might try to interrupt Mary's account of something that he feels threatening to him, as he would have done in all of their previous attempts to discuss it with each other. But on this occasion the counselor can help each of them to get a good hearing by waggling a finger in this case at John, and saying, "Let her have her say, John, and then you can have the floor!" In this kind of manner he can keep the discussion from being swamped by the emotional components in the disorder.

Under such good-natured control the particular grievance will be hammered out to some kind of mutual agreement, and then the counselor, who has shown full acceptance of the atti-

tudes and behavior of each of them, can take up any such matter with the partner concerned in a subsequent individual
interview. For example he might say to "John," "What about
those outbursts of cruelty that Mary brought up when you
were both here last time? What sort of thing gets in your hair
to stir you up in that way?"

From this point the counselor may be able to work with
John backwards towards any frustrated role expectations, his
habitual attitudes and responses, his uncritical assumptions,
emotional needs and their frustrations, and also his childhood
experiences with parents and others which might well provide
him with the clues to the violent reactions which perplexed
him as much as they upset his wife.

Properly handled, such joint interviews can make the rest
of the counseling move ahead in such cases as these, by bringing many important areas of conflict on to the "agenda."

A second and generally later reason for joint interviewing
is that when each partner has achieved reasonable insight it
still may be a valuable way of clearing up many matters of
mutual involvement, or offering appropriate information applicable to both of them, about some of the principles of
personal relationships. These may be termed "mediational interviews," as distinct from the "clarifying joint interviews"
already discussed. There will not generally be as much emotional inter-relationship or interaction in the mediational interviews as in the clarifying ones, and there will be more
constructive and practical discussion.

At this point it is necessary to formulate the main conditions which need to be satisfied if a joint interview is to have
the best chance of succeeding. It goes without saying that the
willingness of both partners is necessary, and the additional
willingness of each of them to bring up any matters which con-

cern them is advisable. But there are some other quite important conditions.

From what has been discussed so far it seems clear that any joint interview is more likely to be helpful if it is left until the emotional tensions have largely subsided. If things become so heated in any joint interview as to be likely to hurt or humiliate either partner too greatly it may be wise for the counselor tactfully to terminate it, either by stopping the whole interview with a sympathetic gesture to each partner, or by suggesting that one of the partners retires for a time and the other (possibly the more hostile one) carry on with an individual interview in which he is encouraged to unburden his intense feeling.

So that the emotional tensions may have a chance of subsiding before any joint interview it is generally wise to have at least two or three individual interviews with each partner before arranging it. Another condition, more difficult to carry out in many cases, is that the counselor should have reasonably comparable rapport with each of the partners. If this is not achieved it is likely that the partner with whom there is less rapport will feel ill at ease and even "odd man out," and that may well do more harm than good. In such cases a more intensive counseling with the partner with less rapport may be very helpful.

CHAPTER VIII

Questions of Appraisal, Referral, and Extended Counseling

1. APPRAISAL

THIS IS A BETTER word than "diagnosis," because it suggests the consideration of the many and varied complex factors in the disorder, and also the assets and liabilities of the partners regarding possible solutions of the conflicts.

As the interviews with each partner and any joint interviews proceed the counselor will be almost automatically arranging the facts and feelings presented to him in some kind of evolving pattern. He will also be assessing the various elements of the trouble, and the capacities of the two partners to deal with the situation and to make use of the counseling. It is vital that he make no attempt to disclose his assessments to the partners, because they are necessarily tentative in any case and open to continuing modification, and also because the partners would generally not be at all receptive of such disclosures. If he is pushed for some assessment it is generally possible to turn the question back by asking how the partner or partners feel about it.

As Dr. Paul Tournier has wisely pointed out in his book "A Doctor's Casebook in the Light of the Bible" (S.C.M. Press, Ltd., London, 1954), there are two diagnoses in any illness.

The first is objective, made by the doctor from the data given to him, and ascertained by his examination and from special investigations. The second is subjective, made only by the patient, with help if need be through the quality of the doctor-patient relationship. Such inner feelings as resentment, guilt, anxiety, pain, love and hostility can be suspected but never adequately assessed by anyone but the person in whom they operate, and this subjective diagnosis or "insight" cannot be imposed or even conveyed to people in emotional disorder from outside.

Apart from this "automatic" arranging of the partners' experiences and feelings about them and about each other it is often important for the counselor to pause at times, in and between interviews, to make a more detailed appraisal of the situation so far revealed to him. He can do this more clearly if he has in mind certain particular aspects on which it can be based.

a. *The personal qualities and attitudes of each partner.* One of the most important matters to consider, particularly when the partners are still living together, is whether either one can stand up to the conflicts for long enough for the counseling to have time to become effective. In many cases a partner will decide this for himself or herself and if it seems unbearable will walk out. But in some cases "walking out" is practically either impossible or appears too drastic to contemplate, and yet one partner may be on the verge of a breakdown in health or emotional balance. In such cases it may be of urgent importance for the counselor to refer that partner to a doctor for help, or to take some quite directive measures to avert a possible catastrophe. People under extreme stress often show quite surprising stamina, but there seems no adequate reason why anyone should be exposed to stresses which might prove too great for him to cope with.

Similar considerations might sometimes apply when it appears that any of the children are being exposed to extreme stress or danger. This may be difficult to assess from hearing the partners' stories, and there is always some tendency for children to suffer from the conflict to some considerable extent. Here again when there is any suspicion of over-severe stress medical help should be considered, or in some cases when available the help of a social worker or a minister.

Apart from the risk of possible breakdown the counselor may well try to assess the capacity of each partner for reasonable insight through further counseling, and for avoiding desperate impulsive actions which might ruin the chances of reconciliation. Assessment of such matters will help the counselor to decide how much counseling to offer either partner, and whether any immediate referral is advisable. For example a partner who seems to be suffering from paranoid delusions is not likely to have any adequate capacity for insight, nor is any partner who may seem to be suffering from any psychoneurotic, psychotic or psychopathic personality type. A psychiatric referral is generally advisable in such cases, if possible through the partner's own doctor.

Other important matters for personal assessment are concerned with attitudes to sex, to personal relationships (possessive, dictatorial, judgmental, over-dependent, aloof, or over-sentimental), to parental attitudes, and to religion. Questions of rigidity or flexibility, and rationality and irrationality may be considered in all these aspects of personal attitude, and the general intelligence and maturity of each will come under some assessment, together with general sensitivity and vulnerability.

As before it must be emphasized that any such appraisal is entirely tentative, and that it is not disclosed to either partner. It is constantly kept under review and modified with each further revelation in the counseling. In some cases the partner's insight may be helped by a question such as, "Does your violent reaction to your wife's remark suggest that you have a vulnerable point there?" and possibly later, "Did you ever have any experience like that as a youngster?"

b. *The quality of the relationships between the partners.* This may show many emotional elements which are not seen in the attitudes of either partner to people other than the marital partner. Many a person shows the most charming manners and the most thoughtful consideration to everyone else but his marital partner. There are many emotional reactions which seem to be brought about by the very fact that the two people are "tied together" in marriage, a tie which may be resented as an "interference with freedom" even though it was accepted willingly and even with intense desire in the first place.

The relationships, for purposes of assessment, may be thought of as personal, sexual, parental, and sometimes specifically religious, for example in a "mixed marriage." Questions of compatibility, cooperation and love can be considered in these fields, together with such matters as role perceptions in marriage, role expectations and consequent role frustrations. Such assessment will give the counselor some valuable data on which to base his continuing management of the counseling or his referral.

c. *Environmental factors in the marital disorder.* While not generally being the most decisive factors these can be strong contributory factors to marital disorder, and it is important for the counselor to give them full consideration in his appraisal of the total situation. It may be that some attention to housing, suitability of neighborhood, suitability of job, influence of "in-laws," matters of finance and other such environmental factors will help in the reconciliation. Social agencies may be of great help in dealing with some "problem families" in this way.

2. REFERRAL

The essence of marriage counseling is in team work, not only among marriage counselors themselves, but also between them and suitable members of a comprehensive panel of consultants. As already mentioned these consultants are professionally trained people of special competence in an appropriate field related to marriage, who are willing to see clients referred to them, generally at their own professional rooms or offices, under a mutually acceptable financial arrangement.

As we have seen they can be divided into two groups, those who are especially competent in the counseling and psychotherapeutic fields, such as psychiatrists, psychologists, and some pastors and social workers; and those with little or no training or experience in the psychological areas but expert in some limited field such as gynecology, urology, medicine, pediatrics, social casework, law, ethics, religion, vocational guidance or child guidance. Other specialists, in such fields as finance and "home economics" or "domestic science" may have a part in some special cases. As also emphasized these consultants should have some continuous contact with the marriage counseling agency with which they work, and some acquaintance with the principles and goals of the work.

The main reason for referral is that the apparent difficulty for which counseling is sought has some elements in it which are beyond the scope or the training or experience of the marriage counselor, and are within the special competence of the consultant. In this way the counselor can refer the partners to someone known to have the most adequate knowledge and experience for this portion of the situation, and can then use his own experience to help with the marital relationship itself. When there is smooth cooperation between the various members of the "team" the clients will receive the best available total help.

Much referral will naturally be governed by availability of the appropriate consultants, geographically, and from the points of view of finance and time. Marriage counselors are generally aware of the available resources in the community for such consultation, and the conditions on which clients are accepted, and this prevents disappointment and frustration.

The actual process of referral is one which needs careful and tactful handling by the counselor because it may cause some strain to any client who has "summoned up courage" to come originally for the counseling and experienced some rapport with the counselor. The prospect of going over some of the possibly painful material again, and the suggestion that referral means that the situation may be more serious than anticipated, may produce considerable anxiety and even resistance in the client.

It is generally best for the counselor, at some appropriate opportunity in the discussion, to begin with a simple bit of information such as, "This seems to be a little outside my particular field, and I think you could be helped better in this by someone with special knowledge. How would you feel about letting me refer you for some special help in this part of the trouble?" If the client shows any hesitation about accepting the idea, he can be encouraged to verbalize his feelings on the matter, with the full acceptance of them by the counselor. When this is done the client will not be so likely to feel pushed around or rejected by the counselor, and the referral may then proceed more smoothly. It is generally much easier to negotiate a referral for the purpose of obtaining special help in a limited field (such as legal or gynecological) than in the deeper psychiatric field.

Any suggestion that either client may need psychiatric help may stir up hostility and defensiveness, especially when the partner has already said the same thing to him previously. It is unfortunate that such an idea of need for psychiatric help is still commonly regarded as a slur on a person's character, and it is generally safer for the non-medical counselor to suggest the need for "medical help" which may be more readily accepted, and the doctor can easily recommend psychiatric help if he thinks fit. In any case it is best to refer anyone needing any kind of medical help in the first place to his own doctor.

What kinds of trouble might be referrable for psychiatric help through the client's own doctor or some physician of his choice? In some cases the need is quite obvious. Completely irrational delusions, depression that shows any possible risk of suicidal tendencies, the over-enthusiasm that goes beyond reason and involves the risk of spending far too much or doing without sleep, which is characteristic of mania, the complete inappropriateness of feeling or action of the young schizophrenic, and any other kind of mental attitude or social behavior that may be harmful or obviously irrational. Any sexual problems which do not respond to simple counseling are also best referred in this way.

Some people show quite intense psychic symptoms such as deep moody depression at home, but seem to be able to carry on a responsible job and to get on reasonably well with their associates. In fact they can be natural and gracious with everyone else, but utterly ungracious with their marriage partner. This suggests some deep elements of hatred or jealousy, or morbid guilt, and such conditions may respond very well to more prolonged counseling. But if they do not seem to respond to some extent with the achievement of rapport they may be better referred, especially if the counselor has not had much experience.

Among the less obvious referrals we may think of the less seriously depressed people who may yet be greatly and quickly helped by special psychiatric treatment and are not helped by prolonged discussion, and the obsessed who are also more often harmed than helped by repeated discussion of their feelings and urges. We may also include the various forms and manifestations of psychopathic personality, already mentioned in the chapter on contributory factors in marital disorder. People with extreme and persistent anxiety, indecisiveness, phobias, and over concern with an incessant variety of symptoms may also be referrable when their troubles are getting in the way of marital cooperation, but it is not always necessary that neurotic trends should be dealt with unless the sufferer wishes to do something decisive about them. Neurotic elements in husband and wife may even balance one another well in marriage, to such an extent that any radical change in one of them may even injure the whole balance and bring unhappiness to both partners.

Finally among the psychiatric referrals we may include any case in which the counselor feels that in spite of the fact that a client's statements are plausible, coherent, and sincere it is difficult to make adequate sense out of them, or possibly to decide whether there may be a delusional element in them. Such people and any which the counselor is unable to "sort out" are best referred. Anyone who develops undue dependence on the counselor should also be considered for referral.

There are some important ways in which any referral can be made most effective. It is important in the first place to give all the possibly relevant facts that are known about the client and his situation, but the counselor should be sparing about his opinions. It is also helpful to the consultant when the counselor states what has been so far attempted and with what result, and when he can give any other information about the client's background and relationships.

The counselor should state in referring what is being requested from the counselor: appraisal for help in further counseling or further referral, or the total care and further treatment of the trouble by the consultant, with or without continuing participation by the counselor. It saves possible disappointment if the counselor does not "build up" the consultant by such remarks as "He will put you right in no time!" A simple statement that the consultant is regarded as the most suitable person from whom to seek this help is enough.

In many counseling agencies consultants have been of great help in many cases which do not necessarily involve referral of the client in person to them. They can often suggest a helpful line for the counselor to take in a discussion of the case on the telephone, which is often effective and less time consuming for the consultant. Discussions of this kind also help the consultants and counselors to come to know each other better and achieve better team work. They also provide a valuable alternative resource in cases in which the desired referral is either impracticable because of distance time or finance, or because of the unwillingness of the client to visit the consultant.

In the larger counseling agencies in some countries it has been found helpful and practical to have psychiatrists regularly visiting the counseling center for consulting purposes, and also for general supervision of the counseling work, including case conferences with the counselors and any trainees who may be invited. This again adds greatly to the total efficiency of the work and to the quality of the team work, and it will certainly become more and more the normal practice. Other types of consultant will also be brought into the visiting staff as occasion demands. This naturally makes for much smoother and more effective consultations, but it would only be practicable in counseling agencies of a reasonable size.

3. EXTENDED COUNSELING

After several interviews with one or both partners individually, some joint interviews, and possibly some referral to one or more consultants, the time may be ripe for a careful review of the situation with a view to deciding about the feasibility and value of further counseling. Some counselors make it clear in their defining of the aims and methods of counseling in the early stages that they will give up to a certain number of interviews, and then will review the whole situation with the clients in this way. This has some value, firstly in making sure that the clients realize that their trouble may need more than one or two interviews, and secondly in making them aware that they cannot leave everything to the counselor and take little active part themselves.

In discussing the conditions which affect the decision for extended counseling and the possible ways and methods of conducting it we face a practical difficulty. Every case is essentially unique, and it is quite impossible to chart out the whole process of counseling. Even if a complete verbatim case record were taken from tape recordings it would not necessarily be of sufficient help in other cases, and it would take up much more space than would be justifiable in this book even if the author had access to any such tape recordings. An attempt has been made so far to provide a reasonable account of the actual work of marriage counseling and to give summaries of portions of the discussion of some common problems, and we are now to consider some of the criteria and methods of extended counseling, to be decided at the time of reviewing the individual case after a reasonable amount of counseling. This can be attempted by considering some alternative situations.

In the first place, if the counseling seems still to be proceeding satisfactorily and some progress is being made, it would generally seem right to go on and to give the situation more time to work out. Any ideas about how much time might be required are necessarily arbitrary, and as long as the clients feel that they are being helped enough to warrant continuation there would seem to be no reason for stopping. It often takes considerable time and patience for deep wounds to heal, and for some of the more "difficult" realities of the situation to penetrate sufficiently into the obstinate minds of many people to enable them to face the difficulties honestly and work through them into a new and more realistic chapter of their marital enterprise.

A second kind of situation is that in which the clients, or at least one of them, are willing to go on, but the counselor has some doubts of the efficacy of further counseling. It may be that one or both are repeating the same old complaints or making the same unreal demands, and apparently just using the counseling as an opportunity for unproductive self assertion. The counselor will of course "reflect" this back by asking appropriate questions, such as, "You're still insisting that your wife must do what you want in this in spite of all your acceptance of her need to live according to her own conscience, and we have been into some of your background reasons for your attitude. How would you think I can help you further in this?" Or in the case of an incurably suspicious wife, "You still can't accept his repeated assurances that he's "playing the game" with you. How can I help you in further counseling?"

The counselor is not necessarily put off by such apparent "stalemate" situations, even when his efforts to find out why the client persists in such attitudes appear fruitless. He may be able to help the other partner to better ability to accept the unreal demands, complaints and suspicions without necessarily acceding to them, so that the partners may come better to "agree to differ" without the necessity of continued destructive and mutually distressing conflict. Time heals many things if given enough chance, and we may remind ourselves that many partners have a greater "vested interest" in staying together, even with constant quarreling, than they are ready to admit to the counselor or to each other.

A third kind of situation is that in which one partner seems to be suffering from a condition for which no treatment is likely to give any great relief. It may be that the counselor has a psychiatric report to the effect that the best that can be done is to keep the person under reasonable observation, with hospital or institutional care available if there is any "relapse" or other difficulty. People who are haunted by fixed delusions come into this category, and so do some of the psychopathic personalities. They may provide a difficult problem for the counselor, but he is often in a different situation from that of the professional psychotherapist. In dealing with the relationship rather than the intra-personal dynamics of the partners he may still be able to help some apparently "hopeless" cases to make a better job of ordinary living than he realizes, as long as either partner will cooperate with his efforts.

If the counselor allows himself to feel defeated in the face of apparently incurable psychic illness which is yet mild enough for a person to be able to live outside institutions he may deprive the sufferer of some valuable support which could make him easier to live with. He might also deprive the partner of the sick person of some greatly needed support and help in the difficult and distressing task of living with such a mentally ill person.

A counselor's pessimism and defeatism will certainly be felt by the clients, who are then denied the uplift of spirit which would often make the difference between the success and failure of their courage and endurance. This may well be the last real opportunity such clients may have of receiving such a "spirit transfusion," and it is one of the great strengths of good counseling that it often inspires one or both partners to face a grim and unpleasant reality after exploring all possible alternatives, and to achieve a courageous acceptance of an "incurable" partner as he is.

It is an interesting and gratifying fact of life that in some cases, when such an "impossible" partner comes to feel accepted as he is, without any more pressure on him to change, he may, by some strange perversity, begin to grow and to change. The greater their experience the more cautious marriage counselors will be in giving up hope for any marriage, and this optimistic attitude of mind will add much to their influence on their clients.

This may happen particularly in some less obviously "incurable" cases such as alcoholics, who provide their partners with many extra burdens. In most countries the most helpful organization known as "Alcoholics Anonymous" is available to help alcoholics of either sex to "stay sober," and there are increasing clinical psychiatric facilities being developed to help them to discover and to deal with the underlying personality disorder. In most countries there is also an organization associated with "A.A." in which the wives of alcoholics can receive much support and help in handling their difficult situations, and these bodies put out simple literature with suggestions from their experience. The partners of mentally ill people also need help of this kind, and it may be a valuable part of marriage counseling services to give such support and practical help to the partner in handling the problem so as to promote the most comfortable conditions for everyone including the children.

The decision of the counselor about extended counseling may often be helped by discussion of the whole case at a case conference of counselors and possibly consultants as well. His own resume of the case will clarify it in his own mind and the comments of his colleagues and some of their questions will often open up a previously overlooked aspect of the case. But ultimately the decision must be made by the counselor himself, and if he does not feel disposed to go on, it must be conveyed to the clients in terms and attitudes which will not appear "rejecting." Fortunately this does not very often arise. Many of such clients will realize the situation and terminate the counseling on their own initiative.

If the counselor allows himself to be committed to extended counseling, there are various ways in which it can be carried out. As we have seen the counselor may often help greatly in a supportive and educative role once the main emotional components of the disorder have been sufficiently ventilated. The supportive role may be necessary for a time simply because the client may have nobody else to turn to. It may be an essential part of this extended counseling to encourage such clients to look for other resources in the community for support, such as a church, or a social or cultural or "handcraft" group, or even a part time or full time job where practicable. It is the essence of counseling to help people to help themselves and to overcome any dependency which may be unavoidable for a time.

The educative role of the counselor may also be productive for the clients in extended counseling. Education and healing cannot be separated, and even in the healing of physical illnesses the patient often needs to be educated regarding the main principles of healthy living, diet, rest and exercise, and general hygiene. Many disturbed marital partners can be helped by some good education in the principles of personal relationships, in matters concerning sexual attitudes and in problems of parenthood.

One aspect of the educational part of counseling which applies at this point more appropriately than in the earlier stages is the use of suitable literature, typewritten material, pamphlets, booklets, magazines, and books. In such cases it is often helpful to offer the opportunity of discussing anything in the literature supplied with the counselor, as referred to in a previous chapter. Lectures may also have a place in some cases, especially when they are accompanied by group discussion.

In some stubborn cases there may be an important part for some kind of group counseling, an activity which is beginning to develop more in recent years. It may include "unstructured" group discussion, "role-playing" in conflicts felt by any members of the group, including the reversal of the conflicting roles, and also "psychodrama" in which specific questions and problems as well as those experienced by members may be acted out under the supervision of the counselor or a trained therapist. It is probable that there will be a steady expansion of such methods of counseling and psychotherapy in the future.

With extended individual counseling the two most common questions for the counselor to decide concern the dependency of the client and the possibility of the counseling extending more deeply into psychotherapy. He can guard against undue dependency by continually throwing the initiative and responsibility back on the client, suggesting some specific "home work" between sessions, either thinking out some particular aspect of his problem or carrying out some project designed to improve the home conditions, or whatever seems appropriate for his further development. He can also increase the time between counseling sessions, so that more responsibility lies on the partners to work things out, even at the risk of more wounds. By accepting the client's feelings of cynicism and encouraging the client to work through them he is also guarding against undue dependency.

In extended counseling if the counselor goes beyond supportive and educational counseling to persist with attempts to elicit the deeper underlying factors in the partners' attitudes he will probably find himself drawn into deeper individual psychotherapy than he may have allowed for. His handling of this will depend partly on his own training and experience in the conduct of deeper counseling, and partly on the availability of resources for individual psychotherapy.

He can decide his course of action better if he can honestly assess his own limitations, how "comfortable" he feels in the counseling and above all in the handling of transference and any of the other mental processes described in an earlier part of this book. If possible it may be well to consider further referral, or at least discussion in a case conference, but if he is committed to carrying on and can handle any transference or dependency without becoming involved he will generally do no harm and might do a great deal of good. His prolonged counseling may provide the necessary time and the right atmosphere for the client to grow steadily in maturity and to achieve gradually improving insight into the deeper elements of the trouble and into the realities of his situation.

If he can keep constantly in the foreground the constantly understood, but not always verbally expressed question to each partner, "What can you offer toward a better partnership, irrespective of your partner?" it will tend to keep a practical and constructive orientation to the discussions.

In some cases extended counseling may be conducted with one or both partners right through the experience of separation or even divorce. This is an experience in which either partner and probably the children, will need some help, and this aspect of counseling will almost certainly develop greatly in the future. It needs to be realized by the clients from the beginning and by the public always that no reputable marriage counselor would have any "vested interest" in trying to induce two unwilling partners to stay together, however foolish he may think they would be to give up the attempt to work things out. He may look with each of them at the reasons for their decision and at the possible consequences to themselves and the children, but the ultimate decision is in their hands and the counselor respects their freedom to make it completely, and goes on accepting each of them whatever they may decide.

In some cases the counselor will have the opportunity of interviewing the "co-respondent" or the third element in a triangular situation, and the same acceptance holds there too, with a full encouragement for ventilation of all feelings in the matter. In many cases this accepting relationship is felt deeply, in contrast to the condemnatory attitudes of all kinds of other people, even though it is realized that acceptance does not mean that the counselor condones the action in any way. In such an atmosphere the defenses may go down and the "third party" may be able to look better at the long term implications of what is being contemplated, and then to set out to encourage the re-establishment of the partnership. This has happened in a number of cases.

In all counseling the situation ultimately has to be faced that marriage must always involve some sacrifice of individualism, some genuine readiness to give as well as to take, to look beyond one's own concerns and to consider and care enough for those of one's partner to be willing to make reasonable adjustment to them, whether the partner seems to be considerate or not.

Until the two partners can learn to think in terms of "we" rather than of "I," until their marriage itself comes to receive some reasonable priority in the scale of values of each partner as a creative joint project worthy of the best that each of them can offer to it, they will fail to derive the satisfaction and growth of personality that marriage, more perhaps than any other relationship, can give them. It is such a conviction as

this which animates and sustains all efforts of marriage counselors to hold fast to their work even through times of great
difficulty and doubt. But the results are constantly confirming
their inner convictions and strengthening their staying power.

In conclusion it may be stated that with all its trials and
difficulties marriage counseling is the most rewarding work,
constantly strengthened by the awareness of its creative results.
The regular renewal and re-creation of threatened, disturbed,
and even broken marital partnerships, and the realization that
the benefits which come from this healing work go on through
the children into the next and future generations, produce
in marriage counselors a steadily deepening devotion to
their high calling, which is further inspired by the com-
radeship and team work between them.

There can be few healing works which can promise such
consistent and far reaching benefits to people and to the whole
community, and we shall probably come to realize that in the
underpinning and healing of home and family life, the greatest
of all possible contributions is being made to the prevention
of mental, social and even much physical illness, and still better
to the promotion of total health, in the best sense of that term,
in the communities of the world. It is hoped that this book
may in some small way add its contribution to the personal and
community welfare in this important and growing field of
creative service.